The
Archangel
Guide
to the
Animal World

The
Archangel
Guide
to the
Animal World

DIANA COOPER

HAY HOUSE

Carlsbad, California • New York City • London
Sydney •Johannesburg • Vancouver • New Delhi

First published and distributed in the United Kingdom by:
Hay House UK Ltd, Astley House, 33 Notting Hill Gate, London W11 3JQ
Tel: +44 (0)20 3675 2450; Fax: +44 (0)20 3675 2451; www.hayhouse.co.uk

Published and distributed in the United States of America by:
Hay House Inc., PO Box 5100, Carlsbad, CA 92018-5100
Tel: (1) 760 431 7695 or (800) 654 5126
Fax: (1) 760 431 6948 or (800) 650 5115; www.hayhouse.com

Published and distributed in Australia by:
Hay House Australia Ltd, 18/36 Ralph St, Alexandria NSW 2015
Tel: (61) 2 9669 4299; Fax: (61) 2 9669 4144; www.hayhouse.com.au

Published and distributed in the Republic of South Africa by:
Hay House SA (Pty) Ltd, PO Box 990, Witkoppen 2068
info@hayhouse.co.za; www.hayhouse.co.za

Published and distributed in India by:
Hay House Publishers India, Muskaan Complex, Plot No.3, B-2,
Vasant Kunj, New Delhi 110 070
Tel: (91) 11 4176 1620; Fax: (91) 11 4176 1630; www.hayhouse.co.in

Distributed in Canada by:
Raincoast Books, 2440 Viking Way, Richmond, B.C. V6V 1N2
Tel: (1) 604 448 7100; Fax: (1) 604 270 7161; www.raincoast.com

A catalogue record for this book is available from the British Library.

ISBN: 978-1-78180-660-9

Interior images: 1 Carol Cavalaris; 25 Galyna Andrushko/shutterstock;
169 Willyam Bradberry/shutterstock; 201 Jay Ondreicka/shutterstock;
219 Chaikovskiy Igor; 249 Chuyuss/shutterstock; 267 Andreas Zerndi/
shutterstock; 287 Wayne Lawes; all other images Oleg 1969/shutterstock

Contents

Contents

Introduction

The Creatures of Our Planet

When the angels sent me my gorgeous Papillon Jack Russell, called Venus, she opened my heart to all animals and changed my life. A year later a small grey tabby called Ash-ting (now a large grey tabby) came into our home and animals became a huge part of my journey.

The angels started to remind me that when animals incarnate on Earth they are undertaking a soul mission just as humans are. Since the fall of the civilization of Atlantis most of humanity has been living at a third-dimensional frequency, which means that they vibrate slowly from ego and selfishness. Over recent years more have opened their hearts and recognized that they are on an eternal soul journey, which has moved them into the fourth dimension. And now humanity is beginning to embrace the fifth dimension, caring for the highest good of all. Many animals are highly evolved, and by 2014 74 per cent had reached a fifth-dimensional frequency where their vibration has speeded up because they are operating from an open heart. At that time only 58 per cent of humans had done so.

Every animal comes to experience life on this physical plane. Like humans they are here to feel the coolness of water or the wind on their body, to touch a leaf, to taste food, to understand sexuality, and what it is like to be a parent and care for another creature, to relate to each other and other species and to other creatures, as well as to take care of the natural world. These are the experiences of every single being on this planet. It is meant to be a joint adventure and involves participation between humans, animals, insects, trees, elementals and all sentient beings.

Before an animal species is allowed to incarnate on Earth, their oversoul, which is the aspect that takes collective decisions for them as a whole, makes a sacred contract with Source, or God, and Lady Gaia, who is the ninth-dimensional angel in charge of Earth, about their mission here. In addition, every animal, just like every human, receives a personal invitation from Lady Gaia before they are conceived and reaffirms their holy agreement at that time.

For many years these binding commitments were honoured. Humans were the guardians and protectors because they were left-brain orientated and were able to plan. This was always intended to be undertaken for the highest good of all in alignment with the divine heart and mind.

No animals agreed to let humans eat their flesh or imprison or ill-treat them.

Because we violated the sacred trust there will be repercussions, for animals are no longer prepared to let themselves be treated in this way. They will withdraw their support unless we change.

Animals have raised their frequency so much in comparison with humans that they are now stepping forward to teach us, and the balance on Earth must shift.

The souls of animals, like the souls of humans, come from different stars or planets, even from different universes. There are currently four planets, stars and constellations that are helping Earth to ascend and these are known as the ascension planets, stars or constellations. Souls coming in from other parts of the universes, including those of animals, must come to Earth via one of these: Neptune, Orion, the Pleiades or Sirius. Here they receive training, so that they are prepared for conditions on Earth and step down their frequency so that they can experience life here.

Just as we have chakras or spiritual energy centres that take in and transmute energy, so too does the cosmos. Each of the stellar ones has an aspect that has already ascended into the higher dimensions. When our chakras become fifth-dimensional we can link them to the cosmic equivalent, which are as follows with their ascended aspects.

- Earth Star chakra links to Neptune and its ascended aspect Toutillay.

- Base chakra links to Saturn and its ascended aspect Quishy.

- Sacral chakra links to Sirius and its ascended aspect Lakumay.

- Navel chakra links to the Sun.

- Solar plexus chakra links to Earth and its ascended aspect Pilchay.

- Heart chakra links to Venus.

- Throat chakra links to Mercury and its ascended aspect Telephony.

- Third eye chakra links to Jupiter and its ascended aspect Jumbay.

- Crown chakra links to Uranus and its ascended aspect Curonay.

- Causal chakra links to the Moon.

- Soul Star chakra links to Orion.

- The Stellar Gateway chakra links to Mars and its ascended aspect Nigellay.

Earth, Orion, Neptune, Sirius and the Pleiades are working cooperatively together to help each other ascend. Because we on Earth have the gift of free will, which for aeons we have used unwisely, our frequency is lower than that of the other planets, stars and constellations. In addition, Earth is the solar plexus chakra of this universe, so we take in and transmute fear and negativity from other planes of existence. This too has kept our frequency down. So the Angels and Masters of Orion, Neptune, Sirius and the Pleiades are doing their utmost to pull us up.

One of the ways they help us is to send animals who come from their domains to Earth, encoded with the energy we need to ascend. The information coded in their aura, the electromagnetic energy field round their physical body, triggers us with what we need for our advancement.

Like many humans they often find the energies very challenging. They too go through the Veil of Amnesia so they experience life on Earth without the advantage of remembering their spiritual selves and their divine connections. And when they die they return to their home planets, taking in their energy fields all that they have learned on our extraordinary planet to enhance the understanding, consciousness and enlightenment of the beings there.

While humans are here using their left brains and their minds, animals are experiencing with their right brains and their hearts. They are much closer to angels and the spiritual world but they don't have the logical, calculating capacity of humans.

Some animals incarnate in service to humanity, others to serve the planet and yet others to experience and grow spiritually through life on Earth. Many are here to teach and to learn. They teach by demonstrating their specially developed qualities. Once a soul is accepted for an Earth mission, they must reincarnate again and again until they have totally fulfilled what they set out to do. Animal souls are no exception so this is why our pets come back to us again and again and there is often a feeling of great familiarity with them. People often remark, 'I feel I've known my horse forever', or 'I'm certain that my cat and I have been together before'. The angels work tirelessly to ensure that the right pet and human meet at the correct time. This is why we are often called upon to exercise patience and wait for the perfect companion to join us. However, the cosmic computer is vast, very complex and all-encompassing.

Experiments on Earth

There have been many experiments and a variety of civilizations over millions of years on Earth.

Since Earth was formed the Intergalactic Council, the group of 12 beings who take decisions for the universe, has run many experiments here. For example, an early experiment was set in Africa to determine if those participating could enable the land to glow with light. This resulted in the Golden Age of Petranium. Animals of diverse shapes were sent to Africa to see how they fared in the conditions there. There have been many experiments taking place over millions of years all over the world. There have also been a variety of civilizations.

When I look at a rhinoceros, I think of dinosaurs. This is not just because of their prehistoric appearance but because they carry memories and information from the Golden Age of Mu, the Age after Petranium, when the dinosaurs roamed the planet. The pelicans of the bird kingdom also hold this information in their energy fields and spread it.

The Wisdom of the Golden Age of Mu

Mu was the era during which the dinosaurs roamed the Earth. The 'people' of Mu were etheric beings and never took physical bodies. Nevertheless, they tended trees and plants, loved the land and the mountains and had a great connection with the four ascension planets, stars and constellations, Neptune, Orion, Sirius and the Pleiades.

Each of these celestial bodies has a chakra in the middle of it. The centre of Earth, known as Hollow Earth, is a seventh-dimensional paradise where all the knowledge and wisdom of Earth is stored within a great pyramid. I describe it in detail in *The Keys to the Universe*. In addition, every being that has ever incarnated, every Golden Age and civilization is represented in etheric form within Hollow Earth. Nothing is lost forever.

Great love and wisdom is held in the chakras in the centres of Earth, Neptune, Orion, Sirius and the Pleiades. The beings of Mu are still holding all this love and wisdom within a healing blue-aquamarine flame of Mother Mary and Archangel Michael in the Hollow Centre of Earth. They also hold the divine blueprints of these five Ascension stars, planets and constellations within the Great Pyramid of Hollow Earth.

Atlantis

The best known and the longest-lasting era is the civilization of Atlantis, which endured in total for 260,000 years. The loose ends of this era were finally tied up in 2012. During this time there were five experiments or tests and the first four were eventually aborted due to misuse of power. However, the fifth experiment produced the Golden Age of Atlantis and was different from all the others.

At the start of the fifth age, the final experiment, a great dome was placed over the land so that the trial was controlled. No person or animal could enter or leave, and in that way the research by the Intergalactic Council was uncontaminated.

It was then that the glorious fifth-dimensional Golden Age of Atlantis developed and the era lasted for 1,500 years. Many animals incarnated to offer themselves in service or to teach and learn. Among these were horses, cows, cats, dogs, sheep and goats.

Humans are also animals. We have taken control, often by using the energy of very generous animals, such as horses or cows, to give us more power. We have expanded our scientific understanding by experimenting on gentle and loving creatures. The way we treat animals profoundly affects their lives and their spiritual growth. Currently what we do to animals, how we think about them and use them is holding back the ascension of the entire planet. Of course, it is also deeply affecting our own spiritual growth. It is time to change.

By working with the information in this book you can connect more deeply with the creatures on this planet. You can also profoundly help them as well as your own evolution.

PART I

~

ANIMALS AND NATURE

Chapter 1

The Spiritual Evolution of Animals and Nature

During the Golden Age of Atlantis every person and all the animals were fifth-dimensional and had 12 activated chakras. The 33 petals of their hearts were fully open, radiating Christ Light, and the people and all creatures loved, honoured and accepted each other.

Animals were considered to be creatures of God, the same as humans but with a variety of shapes and different skills and learnings.

Because humans radiated love and harmlessness, all creatures felt totally safe and were naturally harmless in return.

Nature too was harmless, for everyone appreciated and revered all aspects of it. Trees did not need to grow thorns or bear poisonous berries. The fifth-dimensional humans took only the nuts, leaves or firewood that they needed and they thanked the trees for it. In return trees healed, nurtured and protected the people.

Herbs provided all the medicine that was needed to rebalance people and animals and this was also much valued.

Animals freely offered their products or services, knowing that only that which was needed would be taken, and that they would be respected and looked after in return. The exchange of energies was exact and loving.

All animals, including humans and cats, during that time were vegetarian. This meant that cats had a different jaw structure, more like that of the felines of Ancient Egypt. Their claws were only used to climb trees.

At the fall of Golden Atlantis, the frequency devolved from the fifth to the third dimension. In humans and many animals 23 chambers of the heart chakra closed. The ten that remained active were the green petals of the outer heart. These bring uncomfortable lessons of jealousy, anger, greed, sadness, aloneness or any form of negativity that needs to be addressed and overcome. Yes, animals are on an emotional learning curve too.

During this third-dimensional phase people became unfeeling and uncaring, so a disregard for the essence of animals and their needs was generated. This is the stage that the mass of humanity has been experiencing for the past ten thousand years.

Some animals too closed their hearts and became third-dimensional, while others maintained their fifth-dimensional frequency and advanced chakra system to teach us and demonstrate a higher way of life. We discuss these evolved creatures, animals, birds, insects and trees throughout the book.

The next layer of chambers or petals of the heart is pink, and at this stage this chakra is illuminated with love. You may well have seen this beautiful love shining from the eyes of a person or a horse or a dolphin, for example.

Right now, as people and animals are collectively becoming more fifth-dimensional the central petals unfurl and become violet-pink. Those petals in the very centre are pure white and they open to the love of Source. When enough people on the planet reach this wonderful stage, life will become glorious for humans and animals alike as we create once more a fifth-dimensional Garden of Eden. We will once more treat animals in the way they deserve and all will be illuminated by angels.

However, humans are currently in transition between a third-dimensional plane and a fifth-dimensional one. Humanity as a whole has reached the fourth dimension. At this point the eleventh petal of the heart chakra, the first pink one, is starting to open. This happens when people are ready to love, appreciate, honour, respect and understand animals.

This is beginning to happen now and when the eleventh petal of the collective heart of humanity opens to animals, there will be a huge shift in the world consciousness. The fear levels on Earth will start to reduce, to be replaced with love, hope and new enlightenment.

Already we are seeing more programmes about animals on television. Social media is filled with stories about animals and people are really interested in them. Things are definitely beginning to change.

The petals within the chakras of animals are simpler for they do not have the same capacity to hold on to emotions or rationalize that we do. They naturally find it easier to open their fifth-dimensional hearts.

Because we have more complex feelings, some higher petals of our heart chakras are open and active, yet some of the lower chambers still hold lessons that need to be learned.

You may be loving, giving and caring but still hold jealousy in your heart.

Or, if you have been bitten or had another unfortunate experience with an animal in a past life or earlier in this one, you may hold fear, anger or guilt towards them. This will hold the eleventh petal closed and you may well be allergic to all or some animals. Forgiveness, release and opening this petal will dissolve the spiritual cause of this dis-ease.

If you cause an animal to die before its time, even though your intentions are of the best, you will bear karma, *unless* you hand the spirit of the animal over to the angels. The karma you bear is a closing of the heart chakra. So if you have your beloved pet put down always ask the angels to take it over to the spirit realms.

The immune system is a function of the heart chakra. At a spiritual level all allergies are caused by a partial closing of the heart centre. This may have happened in another lifetime but the repercussions continue until you change your heart.

A friend was living in my house with her large, fat cat. I did not like him and I was outraged when he was put on a diet and became a danger to live with. He would run behind me, put his paws round my legs and try to bite when he wanted food, which was all the time. I immediately became allergic to him. My eyes would run and itch when he was around. So I knew I had to change something in me. I sat down quietly and opened my heart to him, sending him love. I did this every day for a week. I also made an effort to greet him and stroke him. To my astonishment, within seven days, my allergy to him, which was thankfully not too deep, disappeared.

You may be holding some upsetting memory at a deep cellular level of which you are completely unaware. It may have been with an insect, a snake, a cat, a bird, even the branch of a tree that fell on you or a loved one. I offer a visualization about opening your heart to animals, but stay open and allow anything that needs to surface to come into your mind during your inner journey.

VISUALIZATION TO OPEN YOUR HEART
TO ANIMALS OR NATURE

1. Find a place where you can be quiet and still.

2. Visualize yourself sitting on a hillside in soft golden sunshine. Birds are singing and all is peaceful. Breathe the pink-gold of harmlessness from your heart into your aura.

3. You become aware of a large cave in the hillside and its welcoming mouth is filled with sunlight.

4. Walk peacefully towards the cave and as you enter see in front of you a spiral with 33 chambers laid out.

5. Starting to walk the spiral, you feel relaxed and safe. You are drawn to one of the chambers. Within it is something you need in order to heal.

6. Open the door and become aware of something that happened in this life or another that is preventing your heart from opening fully to animals.

7. That is past. It is time now to forgive yourself or the animal or both.

8. Breathe the pink-gold light into the chamber until it dissolves the picture and the feelings.

9. Thank the animal and leave a pink rose in the chamber.

10. Walk back along the spiral knowing you are now free.

Chapter 2

Angels Who Work With Animals

These are some of the angels who work with the animal and nature kingdoms.

The Guardian Angels of Animals

Every animal has two guardian angels who look after them and guide them. These angels stand back and witness their behaviour and choices. As long as the animal is safe, they do not interfere. If the creature is unhappy or in danger, its guardian angel will do all that it can to assist. It will try to change the situation. If this is not possible it will whisper to the animal to try to alter its attitude. At the same time, it will liaise with the guardian angel of the perpetrator in an endeavour to change something. Sadly, most humans still do not listen, but this is changing rapidly.

If a pet or farm animal is being mistreated the angels will whisper to the person who is looking after it to act differently. If it is a wild animal the angels will try to influence the offender to change their behaviour, attitude or actions. If this does not

9

succeed and any creature is harmed or killed, the angels record what happens in the Akashic records, which are the files kept of every thought, word and deed of every single individual. Over lifetimes the offender will have to repay appropriate karma. Healing angels will then soothe the soul of the unfortunate animal.

The Angel of Animals, Archangel Fhelyai

At last Earth has earned the right for Archangel Fhelyai, the angel of animals, to return from another universe to help animals. His presence gradually began to be felt after the Harmonic Convergence in 1987 when so many prayers were sent out by humanity that the 25-year period of purification that was forecast in the Mayan calendar began. Many new, luminous beings started to enter at that time in response to the outpouring of energy from people worldwide, and Archangel Fhelyai was one of them.

Archangel Fhelyai is the beautiful, sunshine-yellow, celestial being in overall charge of the animal kingdom. When he is very focused on a project to heal or help his charges he becomes pure white. He has recently arrived from another universe to this one since we have raised our frequency sufficiently to be ready to receive his assistance.

Archangel Fhelyai will always send one of his yellow angels to help an animal if you ask. He will also send one of his angels to whisper to a human who is mistreating any creature.

If enough people ask Archangel Fhelyai to
help the animal kingdom or light a candle
and dedicate it to the welfare of animals,
the situation on Earth will transform in a flash.

Archangel Fhelyai's Retreat

Every archangel has a place in the ethers above the planet that is specially tuned to their energy. Here they feel comfortable and set up their retreats. And they can use the energy of this place as a transformer through which they can step down their energy if they are coming from a higher dimension.

Many archangels have temples or schools or chambers in the inner planes where they teach or give healing.

Archangel Fhelyai's retreat is on Holy Island, Scotland, UK. You can ask to visit him here during meditation or sleep to receive information, healing or initiations into the animal kingdom.

Other Angels Who Help Animals

As well as their guardian angels, Archangel Fhelyai, angel of animals, and his angels, other specific angels and archangels work with various animals and birds. For example, Angels of Peace work through pigeons, doves and ducks; Archangels Michael and Raphael are influencing tigers; Archangel Gabriel is very connected to rabbits. The ineffable Angel Mary is always with pandas. Many of these Archangels are in fact Universal Angels, indicating that they spread their influence across several universes.

In addition, there are many other angels and archangels who look after animals and help them and I discuss these throughout the book as I share information about different species.

Archangel Purlimiek – the Angel of Nature

Archangel Purlimiek is in charge of the entire nature kingdom, a mighty undertaking. He is a blue-green light and appears in a flash to help where nature is threatened. He tries to intercede with the human who is causing the problem. Often when he whispers into someone's ear, that person has a change of heart about their actions.

I was once sent a magnificent photograph of an Orb of Archangel Purlimiek zooming at great speed to prevent a tree being felled. Apparently he arrived in time to whisper to the person who was felling it, who heard and stopped. He had a sudden, unexpected change of mind!

Archangel Purlimiek's retreat is at the Great Zimbabwe, in Zimbabwe, and from here he coordinates the plan for the nature kingdom on Earth.

Archangel Bhokpi – the Angel of Birds

Archangel Bhokpi is in charge of the bird kingdom. He comes from the ranks of the Seraphim and does not have a specific etheric retreat over Earth. His colour is almost transparent, so he can take on any shade he wishes to use.

Archangel Preminilek – the Angel of Insects

Archangel Preminilek is charged with looking after the insect kingdom. He operates on a yellow-green frequency and his etheric retreat is in the mountains in the north of Myanmar.

Many insects are third-dimensional, though a few are in the fourth and fifth. His task is to look after them all, coordinate their service work and help them ascend into the higher realms.

The Portal of Animals

In 2012, at the Cosmic Moment, a huge finger of Source energy touched our planet and triggered the opening of many great portals of light. This great influx of Source light activated the six great Cosmic Pyramids in Mesopotamia, Egypt, Peru, Greece,

Guatemala and Tibet, which then set alight the 33 Cosmic Portals and many others. One of the greatest of these was the awesome portal for animals in Yellowstone, USA.

Yellowstone has started to radiate the most magnificent sunshine-yellow colour, the same shade as Archangel Fhelyai, to help animals everywhere. Most significantly, this energy is touching and changing the consciousness of humanity in regard to animals. This wondrous portal will be fully open by 2032 by which time the way we think of and treat animals will have totally transformed.

You can link into the Yellowstone portal in your meditations and prayers and ask the angels to direct the yellow light where it is needed. This is a massive piece of service work that will help the animals and accelerate your ascension.

Archangel Fhelyai, supported by the light pouring from the Yellowstone portal, is very actively inspiring animals to tune in to their soul missions and to fulfil them, so that they can enter the fifth dimension. He has been spectacularly successful as currently 74 per cent of animals are living at that evolved frequency.

He is encouraging us humans to shift our consciousness about the animal kingdom and helping humanity to open its collective heart towards all our fellow creatures on this planet. This effort is being supported by the many high-frequency light bursts radiating towards Earth at this time.

One of Archangel Fhelyai's angels is immediately assigned to assist an animal if it is in need or if a human asks for it.

As humans act as bridges between angels and the
physical world we are in a very powerful position to
help all sentient beings by asking for angelic help.

Many animals are losing heart because of the way humans have treated them and judged them. They cannot fulfil their soul missions if they have lost the will to live. They need encouragement, love and freedom to be themselves. The angels try to lift their spirits and give them courage.

If an animal is sick Archangel Fhelyai's angels may offer it healing, comfort and support, though, as with humans, they have to stand back if the soul of the creature so dictates, for animals undergo tests and challenges just as we do.

Prayers for Animals

When you send out prayers for animals, Archangel Fhelyai takes them and uses the energy for the highest good. No prayer is ever wasted, and most people have no idea of the good that they do when they send up a spiritual request, however short. Prayers are powerful.

A friend of mine was very concerned about a dog who was owned by one of her neighbours and who was clearly unhappy. The poor creature was being left alone for long periods of time, which is agony for a sociable animal. The neighbour was impervious to her hints, so she decided to talk to Archangel Fhelyai. She lit a candle and told him the problem, then asked him to find a solution. She did this for the highest good of this dog every day for a week. At the end of that time the owner was suddenly made redundant. She was at home with her dog and able to be with him and take him for walks. It was not quite the outcome my friend expected, but we have to let go and allow the angels do what is for everyone's highest good!

The Birth and Death of Animals

Archangel Fhelyai or one of his angels is always present at the birth and death of every animal, however small or humble.

This moment of transition is as important for an animal as for a human. It is the first great initiation for every creature who enters the adventure of Earth.

Naturally, Archangel Fhelyai or one of his angels is also with every animal as they pass over. This is the second most important initiation every animal and human must undertake.

Every soul or group soul is important and is sent an individual invitation by Lady Gaia, the Throne or ninth-dimensional angel in charge of Earth, before they incarnate.

Just like humans, angels love to see a newborn for they still carry pure innocent Source light. If someone calls to see your new kitten, puppy, foal or any other babe, they will bring many angels with them to bless the animal.

Archangel Fhelyai may send an angel to stay with an animal for a few days before their time of passing to help them adjust to the transition and to learn any last lessons they need to understand. If it is a beloved family pet this will help the family to let go too.

Archangel Azriel's angels are also present at the birth and death of every animal. In addition, their guardian angels are with them, holding the light for them and encouraging them.

If an animal dies suddenly they may be in shock and your prayers are very important to help them find the light. When a death is untimely their angels will give them healing and the nurturing they need. Then they will help them to choose new conditions on Earth, so that they can come back to learn the lessons they originally incarnated to experience.

The fifth-dimensional animals, birds and fish cannot die unless they choose to leave. While something may seem like a horrible accident or devastating act, their death is always orchestrated by the angels in conjunction with their higher selves to teach lessons. For example, a dolphin does not get entangled in a net or a turtle eat polythene bags by chance.

These evolved creatures are showing us that we must clean up our oceans. Birds only die in service. A tiger cannot be trapped unless its soul allows it.

When someone does kill an animal the karma is terrible. Where animals are butchered to eat without consideration or prayer, some of the creature's fear is passed to the humans who consume it. Every single person who is involved in some capacity, however small, with the production of meat bears a proportion of the karma.

I believe that, at some level, people know this. When she was about seven one of my granddaughters, who is vegetarian, was friends with a child of the same age who lived opposite them. One day, a big argument ensued on the way to school. The little friend insisted that lamb, pork and beef were not meat. I am not sure what she thought they were but she said that her mother, who was a GP, had told her they were not from animals. The child declared she would never eat an animal and she will have a shock one day when she learns that what my granddaughter told her is true. I guess her mother will carry the karma.

 ## VISUALIZATION TO HELP THE ANIMALS

1. Find a place where you can be quiet and undisturbed.

2. Invoke the wisdom and protection of the Gold Ray of Christ and see the golden light flow down over you.

3. Picture golden roots reaching down from your feet into the earth.

4. Imagine yourself sitting on a hillside overlooking vast plains. The sky is polished azure and the sun a golden-white light. All is peaceful.

5. Suddenly you find yourself surrounded by hundreds of Archangel Fhelyai's sunshine-yellow angels. They are lighting up the world like radiant suns.

6. Each angel is at your service. Command them to help the animals of the world. You may choose a species or particular animals.

7. See rainbow bridges of light flowing from your heart to the animals you want to assist.

8. Be aware of flashes of bright yellow as the angels slide along the rainbow bridges to the animals and surround them in loving, healing, protective yellow light.

9. Archangel Fhelyai himself now brings you an animal. It may be one you know or one you have never seen before. It may be a domestic animal or a wild one. Held within his aura it is calm and loving.

10. Take time to stroke and communicate with this animal. It may have a message for you.

11. Telepathically offer it words of hope and wisdom.

12. Then thank Archangel Fhelyai and his angels and watch them withdraw.

13. Gently open your eyes and know you can help the animals at any time.

Chapter 3

Animal Colourings

The colouring an animal presents with is a soul choice. Markings or overall shades are never by chance. The colours offer information, attract challenges, draw attention to different qualities, give warnings, teach or serve in a number of other ways.

For example, black-and-white animals are generally, but not always, teaching about balance, like a zebra, or guiding you not to go to one extreme or the other, like pandas. And, yes, spots and stripes offer camouflage but they are often chosen for another purpose too.

I have written many times about my beautiful dog, Venus, who is white with one brown ear and a brown marking over her right eye like an Egyptian eye symbol. One day as we lay in bed she told me that she had been my dog in an incarnation in Egypt and she had been a queen dog. She said she had insisted on having this eye marking so that I would recognize who she truly was. Indeed, how could I doubt it? When a friend of mine picks her up and puts her in her bicycle basket she loves it. She sits like a queen with her ears flapping in the breeze as if she is being borne in a litter.

It is the same with humans. Occasionally we read about a black person and a white one having twins, one black and one white. Needless to say this is not by chance. At a soul level they are choosing to call in different life experiences. And puppies born in the same litter with a variety of colourings and markings are making choices to express their soul energy.

Pure White Animals

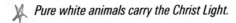 *Pure white animals carry the Christ Light.*

The Christ Light is held in the ninth-dimensional level of Sirius, where it is a pure radiant white, overlit by Source love. The majestic and awe-inspiring unicorns are able to radiate it where it is needed. As the frequency is stepped down, golden angelic energy merges with it so that it becomes the Gold Ray of Christ.

There are three kinds of white animals and all of them are connected with Archangel Gabriel, the pure white archangel, and the unicorns. All carry different levels of Christ Light.

Albino Animals

These animals are born with lack of colour and eye pigmentation. They are very visible to predators and so are more likely to be caught. They often have health problems and poor vision. In addition, their own species tend to regard them as an aberration and often kill them.

At a soul level they carry some Christ Light. Other animals see or sense the light and cannot cope with it, so they try to put it out. The albino animals have to learn to stand out. Their lives are often a sacrifice. This means that their experience on Earth takes them through an initiation. This is a test agreed by their soul. These animals undertake the fourth initiation, which is known as a crucifixion and is one of the most challenging of all. The purpose is to strengthen them spiritually in order to raise their frequency for the next stage of their soul journey. They are preparing to bring in the blazing white Christ Light.

Animals Who Have Adapted to Living in Snow-covered Regions

Wherever there is snow the energy of the land is high and pure and Archangel Gabriel is present. Animals such as polar bears, arctic foxes, snow leopards, arctic wolves, Siberian tigers and arctic seals have adapted to living in the Arctic by developing white fur. Some, like hares and stoats, who become ermine, have the ability to change rapidly to white when the snow arrives.

They are all overseen by and in the protection of the diamond-bright light of Archangel Gabriel. All these animals carry some Christ Light and spread it wherever they go in order to raise the light.

Other Pure White Animals

Pure white animals are being born throughout the world, seemingly normal apart from their white skin and blue eyes.

Normal pure white animals are a
phenomenon of our evolving times. They
all bring in the Christ Light and blaze
it out through their energy fields.

Often they are incarnating on Earth for the first time, in full purity, divine essence and harmlessness. In the main these animals are not being killed.

The first reason is because the consciousness of the animal kingdom has risen so that they can accept the light these beautiful creatures emanate.

Secondly, these pure white animals automatically raise the consciousness of those around them, so their predators move into love energy.

Thirdly, they radiate harmlessness and peace, which confers safety on them.

Evolving White Animals

White Horses

In general, as animals evolve their fur becomes whiter. The higher they progress into the upper levels of the fifth dimension the whiter their fur becomes. If you see a glorious snow-white horse you know it is ready to ascend.

Aleja Fischer, who was a Principal Teacher with the Diana Cooper Foundation, was with her white horse when it died and she saw its spirit rising up and turning into a pure white unicorn. What an amazing experience.

White Lions

When I was writing my spiritual novel *The Web of Light*, based in Africa, I was blessed to see genuine white lions and they are indeed noble, gracious animals. An ineffable quality radiates from them and when you look into their eyes you receive a download of Christ Light. They are heralding the return of the Cosmic Christ energy to Earth.

Swans

These majestic birds demonstrate grace and harmony. They spend much of their time floating on water, which is the element that carries universal love and enables creatures who live in or on it to maintain purity. This helps swans to absorb love and pour out Christ Light in exchange.

Black Animals

Black represents the divine feminine, the deepest levels of mystery and magic. It is where the new is nurtured and kept safe while it develops. It is the colour of secrecy and hiding. Some animals choose to be black as it hides them at night. They are calling in the secrecy of blackness.

Black Cats

In the golden era of Atlantis all the cats were black. They helped to hold the frequency high and they assisted with healing and magical works in the temples. They held the purest and greatest integrity. Even today a black cat holds special energies. Superstition has meant they are considered 'witchy' and some people are afraid of the power they hold.

Brown Animals

Brown, sandy or tawny are earth shades and help animals with these colourings to connect to Mother Earth.

Brightly Coloured Birds

Because birds incarnate with nothing to learn from us, they can choose bright plumage that is the colours that the Archangels radiate. For example, a bright-green parrot will be bringing through Archangel Raphael's emerald light. A rainbow parrot will be reflecting the light of many different archangels.

It is fascinating to see all the different animals and birds, often seemingly the same, but with a huge variety of colours and markings, all chosen for a purpose.

VISUALIZATION TO TUNE IN TO THE COLOURS
AND MARKINGS OF BIRDS AND ANIMALS

1. Find a place where you can be quiet and undisturbed.

2. Ask Archangel Fhelyai, angel of animals, to place his yellow light all round you.

3. Ground yourself into the earth with silver roots.

4. Breathe comfortably, focusing on your heart chakra, until it is pink and white, and glowing.

5. Invite an animal or bird to come to you and wait to see who arrives.

6. Surround it with your beautiful soft pink-and-white heart energy.

7. Sense your hearts connecting and then your souls.

8. Now gently tune in to why this animal chose these markings. What did it wish to express? Did it want to teach? What was its message?

9. Thank it for coming to you and bless it as it leaves you.

10. Open your eyes and reflect on anything you have learned.

PART II

~

THE ANIMAL
KINGDOM

Chapter 1

Aardvarks

Message from the Aardvark Kingdom

*We ask you not to judge or condemn those who have polluted
our planet. When you do so you too add etheric pollution.
Instead we ask you to bless the polluters with love, hope and a
vision of the world clean, pure and at peace. That is the greatest
way you can help us, Lady Gaia and our beautiful Earth.*

The aardvark originates from Sirius and its name means
earth pig in Dutch. It is a nocturnal animal found all over
Africa, and in its quiet way does its own service work, carrying
ancient knowledge from early Atlantis in its energy fields. It
is one of the few creatures that holds for us a memory of the
third experiment of Atlantis.

At that period the continent of Atlantis filled the Atlantic
Ocean and abutted Africa. Two things occurred. Firstly, vast
animals evolved. Massive cats, horses, mammoths and birds
developed. Eventually they overran the world. Secondly,
despite a cornucopia of delight that had been prepared for the
settlers of this third experiment, dissent and disharmony arose
between the people. The Children of the Law of One wanted to
live pure lives in connection with God while the Sons of Baliol

wanted to indulge all their lower passions and senses. The seismic energy that was created allowed in a negative outside influence.

This enabled an entity from another universe to connect with and mastermind these oversized animals. Under this malign influence they became vicious and dangerous. It was difficult for people to survive, let alone live in these conditions so they tried many peaceful methods to deal with the animals. However, nothing worked.

Eventually the famous Five Nation Conference with its fateful outcome was called to discuss the situation. Delegates teleported from all over the world to Atlantis. They were desperate because life on the surface had become almost impossible. With many misgivings, but feeling helpless in the face of this dire situation, they took the monumental decision that has affected Earth ever since. They agreed to set off nuclear bombs underground in the hope of killing these animals.

This caused massive earthquakes in which over the following 2,000 years the animals and all the people on Earth died. The pollution caused by the nuclear explosions is still contaminating Earth and there are many in physical bodies and others in spirit who are working to clear it.

So the aardvarks hold the memories of the consequences of nuclear explosions. At the same time their service work is about cleansing and clearing the pollution of the original atomic detonation that so damaged Earth.

They remind us that anything done to the body of Lady Gaia has a consequence. The result of mining or digging into the Earth, including fracking, inevitably leads to earthquakes, though they may be many years into the future.

In many ways the aardvark is an enigma. It has ears like a rabbit, a tail rather like a kangaroo and a face like a pig. Living underground in extensive burrows that are quite cool it has an almost hairless body, short neck and short legs. This enables it to move through the earth to inhabit comfortable burrows and also to spread its energy.

Archangel Sandalphon connects with it and helps these creatures to root into Hollow Earth for spiritual sustenance and assistance.

Because it is a nocturnal animal, with poor eyesight, it has a highly developed sense of smell and hearing. In other words, its third eye, the psychic chakra in the centre of the forehead, has evolved those senses.

We are what we eat and aardvarks live almost exclusively on fifth-dimensional ants and fourth-dimensional termites from Sirius. While the aardvarks are third-dimensional, the energy bodies of the ants help them to deal with all the contamination that they absorb, transmute and cleanse.

Their work is more important than we realize for it is important to clear the pollution from those Atlantean nuclear explosions before the new Golden Age can really come to fruition. The aardvarks are assisted in their task of cleansing the ancient pollution by esaks, who are tiny elementals who came here from another universe before 2012. Archangels Purlimiek, the angel of nature, and Archangel Butyalil, in charge of Earth's place in the Universe, sent out a clarion call that vibrated throughout the universes for volunteers to help clear the pollution on the planet. These minute winged creatures, a fraction of the size of a fairy, responded. In exchange for experiencing Earth and being able to take back to their home planet all they have learned, they agreed to come here to consume negative etheric energy. They congregate in places where drug use pollutes the atmosphere or toxic waste is dumped or lower vibrations gather and they make valiant efforts to digest the lower frequencies and transmute them through their light bodies. They are wondrous little light workers and since 2012 they have been helping the aardvarks with their extraordinary service missions.

Service Work

Each time you send blessings and love to the aardvarks you are helping them to fulfil their soul mission. At the same time, you are adding your light to the clearance of the pollution from the third experiment of Atlantis.

Prayer to Archangel Fhelyai

Beloved Source and Archangel Fhelyai, angel of animals,

I am sending pure light and love from my heart to the aardvark kingdom and ask that you use this energy to help these animals with their soul mission.

I also pray that blazing white light from the glorious heart of Source flies deep into the Earth to dissolve all lower energies caused by human indiscretion and bring our beautiful planet into her rightful place as a fifth-dimensional paradise.

So be it. It is done.

VISUALIZATION TO CONNECT WITH ARCHANGEL FHELYAI

1. Find a place where you can be quiet and relaxed.
2. Send golden roots into the Earth and call in the protection of the Gold Ray of Christ.
3. You find yourself in a large cool burrow where you feel very safe and comfortable.

4. You are in a magical world surrounded by hundreds of pinpricks of light. These are tiny winged elementals, the esaks.

5. By their light you can see clearly as a friendly aardvark approaches. It is so pleased to meet you and to know that humans are ready at last to help them with their mission.

6. You can see the deep sadness in its eyes as it thinks of the nuclear pollution left after the third experiment of Atlantis caused all life on Earth to die.

7. You nod as you understand what this creature has been carrying in its energy fields for so long.

8. Tell it that you are ready to add your energy to help it.

9. Then visualize an intense pure white shimmering ball of Source light coming down through your aura, through your feet into the core of the Earth.

10. Each ball fills with black contamination and is taken by angels to the moon for thorough cleansing and regeneration.

11. Continue to let as many of these balls of pure Source energy come through you as you feel is right for you today.

12. Then say goodbye to the aardvark and be aware that you have helped each other.

13. As you return to where you started know that you have done a great piece of challenging service work.

14. Accept a ball of pure white shimmering light into your own heart. Then open your eyes.

Chapter 2

Badgers

Message from the Badgers

The whole world is coming into balance and we are helping this process. If someone harms you, send them love and trust that this will soften their hearts. Then they will never harm you, anyone else or any animal ever again. Love is the only way to heal.

B adgers originate from Sirius. They chose at a soul level to be black and white because they wanted to demonstrate the balance between masculine and feminine, the yin yang colours, white for yin and black for yang. So they are learning and teaching about balance.

They are also learning and teaching about family life. A group of six to ten badgers live together in complex underground setts, a system of burrows that they dig themselves, though some are centuries old. Their setts have a number of chambers in them. Some are for sleeping in and in others they give birth and bring up their young.

They dig a number of tunnels leading to the outside world for ease of entry or escape.

These evolved creatures are incredibly clean. They freshen their sleeping rooms and drag old grass, hay or bracken outside to prevent fleas and lice from building up. They never bring food into their homes and they create communal toilets that are placed away from their setts at the borders of their territory.

With their balanced masculine and feminine energy, they look after their young very carefully. The female badger nurtures her cubs lovingly and suckles them for about three months while the male protects the territory.

Badgers choose to live underground because part of their divine mission is to draw into their energy systems and then transmute the negativity that is being held within the Earth. They work with Archangel Sandalphon to help to keep the ley lines, the energetic pathways that link places, clear and in balance and they send light into the Earth Star chakra of the planet and of individuals.

They have well-developed heart centres and the Angel Mary pours pure Source love through their hearts into the planet.

The Angel Mary is trying to hold them in peace and harmony despite all that is happening to them. For centuries they have taken in and transmuted the lower frequencies within the Earth and coped exceptionally well with this spiritual task. However, for the past few hundred years, low-frequency humans have baited and killed these loving, giving creatures. Unsurprisingly this has stressed them. It is almost unbelievable that despite fulfilling their spiritual purpose very competently for ages these beautiful creatures are treated so badly by people.

If you were taunted and baited, you would undoubtedly feel very frightened. Even worse, you might feel that somehow you must be bad and undeserving. Sensitive badgers are the same.

The persecution of badgers has made them vulnerable to TB.
The metaphysical reason for TB is a feeling of unworthiness.

Archangel Uriel is trying to help them build their confidence and regain a sense of worth and importance on the planet. We are all part of the whole. As badgers raise their frequency once more and recognize who they are, so too will humanity.

The greatest way we can help badgers is to send them love and appreciation. This will help them to build their immune system and be healthy once more. It will enable them to fulfil their purpose with joy. When their auras are strong they will find a way to stand up to the bullies and when this happens humans will no longer trouble them.

I was walking along the road when I met a tattooed young man who stopped to talk to Venus. He told me that he had a Staffie, who was the gentlest most loving dog. Apparently he was taking his old dog for an evening stroll round the block when a van stopped and three men threw the Staffie out of it, then drove on. The dog was badly injured, with badger claw marks all over its face and body. He took the traumatized dog to the vet who stitched it up and said he'd been used for badger baiting. When the young man said he'd like to keep the animal and look after it, the vet refused payment. The stranger said he was the best dog he had ever had and was best friends with his little girl who was three. He got out his camera and showed me photos of the Staffie and his daughter. There was an obvious bond of love between them.

I know this is really a story about a dog rather than a badger who was defending itself. But where humans have set animals against other animals, those who have love in their hearts like this young man, can start to heal the situation. The angels orchestrated that he was nearby when the injured Staffie was dumped.

VISUALIZATION TO HELP THE BADGERS

1. Take a moment to breathe comfortably and relax.

2. Picture yourself in a woodland spot just as dusk is setting in.

3. You feel quite safe. Archangel Michael is holding you in his bright-blue protection.

4. You see a badger sett in front of you and one of these beautiful black-and-white creatures pokes out its nose.

5. It senses you are completely harmless so it emerges and ambles towards you.

6. Send a telepathic message to the badger reminding it that it is special and beautiful. Tell it that it is doing a really good job cleansing the planet and can be very proud of itself. Thank it for spreading light and balance wherever it goes.

7. Call in Archangel Fhelyai, angel of animals, and see its yellow light through the trees. Send a rainbow bridge from your heart to the badger and ask Archangel Fhelyai to touch and help the entire badger kingdom.

8. See the badger surrounded in a huge yellow flame.

9. Sense it smiling gratitude to you.

10. Return to where you started, knowing that your energy has helped these beautiful creatures.

Chapter 3

Bats

Message from the Bats

We have much to teach you and we coexist with you in
peace. Please accept us and know that when you develop
the sonar and echolocation techniques that we use, your
world will be a much more evolved and happier place.
Then you will communicate as we do through open heart
and throat chakras and there will only be truth.

Bats originate from another universe, which is why they are often feared and so little understood. They step down through Sirius where they hone their knowledge about sonics and echolocation to fit in with the atmospherics and energy of Earth. They originally practised the use of sonics in Lemuria when they had energy bodies. Some of the species are here to learn about and demonstrate the use of sonics. All of them are learning about birthing and caring for live young. They are also learning and teaching about life and sharing responsibility within a community.

Some are fourth-dimensional for they have developed their heart and care well for their babies. Others are fifth-dimensional.

Archangel Fhelyai, angel of animals, is in overall charge of the bat kingdom but Archangel Dorenka, who is from their universe, oversees them. His frequency is neither faster nor slower than archangels as we understand them. He just vibrates on a different wavelength.

Bats do not need humans or want anything to do with us. They have strong immune systems and this is partly because flying uses a lot of energy and keeps their physical bodies strong. However, a strong immune system is an indication of an open heart-centre and they are developing this in their quest to become fully fifth-dimensional.

Like many creatures, bats are learning and teaching about family life on Earth. Bats have strong family ties and are very nurturing and sensitive to those in their group. They are social creatures and live in large colonies where males and females tend to be segregated except when mating. When they give birth the females form a maternity wing within their community. One very tiny live baby is born at a time. The mother has to fly while pregnant, lactating and feeding, and she carries out her maternal duties devotedly.

One highly evolved trait of the bats that is partly responsible for the way they have adapted to life on Earth is that the mother holds sperm in her body until it is the optimum time for it to fertilize an egg. Only then does she release it. She knows when the time is right by listening to Archangel Dorenka who telepathically imparts the information to her. So babies are born when it is warm enough to survive comfortably and there is prolific food.

Bats in different parts of the world eat different foods. Some bats eat only insects; others frogs, fruit, nectar, blood, pollen and fish. This is to take advantage of whatever food is available in their area. Naturally, they have incarnated in that particular place to experience those conditions and have consequently developed different digestive abilities which affect them accordingly. This is all information that they signed on to accumulate while on Earth in order to take it back to Sirius and subsequently to their home universe.

Bats vary enormously in size. The largest bats are the flying foxes with truly huge wingspans of up to two metres. The world's smallest mammal is the bumblebee bat, so called because it is the size of a bee. Bats account for 20 per cent of mammals on Earth and are learning from a wide range of experiences.

They are the only mammals to fly properly rather than glide and are reminding humans it is possible for us to do so too. In fact, their wings are hands that they have adapted for flight. This enables them to be very flexible!

Some bats use echolocation to navigate and hunt. Others have not developed this skill and rely on smell and vision to find food.

They are highly evolved and as their black colour indicates they hold much universal wisdom as well as divine feminine secrets. Their service is to bring the wisdom and knowledge from Sirius as well as their home universe and disseminate it where they can. They teach us by their actions and through energetic connection. We can learn much from them.

Bats can see in the dark. However most of them use echolocation to navigate and catch insects. This is to demonstrate that there is another way to move about if we develop the right aspects of our brains. A few blind humans have developed echolocation abilities.

Their advanced sonics are a result of their highly developed throat chakras that have evolved under the tutelage of Archangel Michael. All sounds form symbols in the etheric. The high-frequency notes emitted by the bats create awesome sacred geometry and this attracts the angels to sing over them.

This means that wherever they fly they clear lower frequencies and leave a trail of divine feminine wisdom!

Within the throat chakra are developed psychic qualities such as telepathy. When bats evolve into the fifth dimension they connect to Telephony, the ascended part of Mercury, and to the Angels and Masters of the Golden Ray just as humans do when we link our fifth-dimensional throat chakra to that ascended star. At that point their auras, which are currently colourless or black, take on a golden radiance.

Newborn bats, with all their spiritual connections still intact and fresh from the love of Source, do have gold in their auras.

Light holds keys and codes of spiritual information, knowledge and wisdom that it can download to us. Most animals need light in order to activate their pineal gland to allow it to receive the keys and codes of universal wisdom. Dark is the absence of light. Within blackness you can make a pure connection with Source with no interference. This is why most people sleep in a dark cocoon at night with curtains drawn so that we can process all that we have absorbed from the light during the day. When we have transcended our lower mental and emotional limitations we embrace pure Source energy in our sleep.

Bats are also demonstrating that they can use other light sources, such as the moon. Their activity is reduced during full moon while they absorb lunar energy and information. This is then processed during the darkness. Lunar energy contains the qualities of the divine feminine.

The bat is highly sensitive to its surroundings. The Native Americans consider it to be a symbol of intuition, dreaming and vision. It suggests the ability to see through illusion into truth. These are all feminine qualities.

Visualization to Help Bats

1. Find a place where you can be quiet and undisturbed.

2. Invoke Archangel Fhelyai, angel of animals, and see his soft yellow light approaching as he stands beside you.

3. Behind him comes Archangel Dorenka with a yellow-brown energy, carrying a tiny baby bat in his hands.

4. Archangel Dorenka offers you the bat, the size of a bee, and you hold it gently in your cupped hands. Feel how soft and furry it is.

5. Be aware of the gold light flowing from its throat as it makes squeaking sounds.

6. Feel the pure white light from its heart centre connecting with your heart.

7. Thank Archangel Dorenka and return the baby bat to him, to give back to its mother.

8. And be aware of a faint wind passing your face as a much bigger bat flies past you. You know it will never touch you.

9. See with enlightened eyes that it leaves a trail of light containing sonic keys and codes wherever it swoops or flies.

10. And then notice that the angels are singing over you and this large bat. The trails are becoming golden and sparkling and spreading. Wherever they flow they dissolve any lower frequencies.

11. Stay open to any message the bat may want to impart. Then thank it for coming to you.

12. The bat soars away and you feel a new understanding and warm heart towards the bat kingdom.

Chapter 4

Bears

Message from the Bears

You are a truly magnificent being on this planet. Yes, you! So remember who you are and stand tall. Then you can touch others with the knowledge and wisdom you carry in your energy fields. People and animals will honour and trust you. Be happy to walk alone until you attract like-minded others to walk with you.

All bears, whether brown, black or grizzly, are fifth-dimensional and originate from Orion, the constellation of enlightenment and wisdom. Creatures from here know how to use their knowledge for the highest good and by the light in their auras influence others to do the same.

Bears have come to Earth to learn and demonstrate how to use power correctly. When they are in the natural habitat for their species they do this magnificently. Then they have shining radiant solar plexus chakras and work directly with Archangel Uriel, the archangel in charge of the solar plexus, to keep it balanced and golden. Archangel Uriel's hosts of angels of peace take light from the bears' auras and spread it where it is needed.

However, these creatures find it very difficult to maintain their authority and dignity when they are removed from the places in nature where they naturally feel comfortable. When they are captured and shackled or caged their self-worth diminishes and they become dejected. Then their solar plexus chakras become murky. Nevertheless, they still radiate the sacred geometry of wisdom in their energy fields so people and other animals sense this. Archangel Uriel works with Archangel Fhelyai, the angel of animals, to help them and lift their spirits.

Except during their brief courtship periods and when a mother is caring for her cubs, bears are solitary animals. They show us that it is possible to live alone, maintain your equilibrium and master your environment. They do not need any creature outside themselves and are happy in themselves when free.

They spend long periods in hibernation, and during this time in their dark cocoon are held in the ineffable energy of Source. The Masters of Orion also have a very strong link to them and feed them with wisdom energy, especially during these long periods of deep sleep.

Bears are not only connected to Archangel Uriel. Archangel Jophiel, the angel of wisdom, shines his light onto them. His pale crystal-yellow energy links to them and keeps them plugged into the higher love aspect of Orion. Within wisdom there is always love. Archangel Jophiel is then able to connect the hearts of the bears to the hearts of those who are pure enough to accept this love. This especially applies to children and is one reason why children love teddy bears. You only have to think of a bear (or a teddy) and this link to the higher heart of Orion is activated.

Polar bears

The polar bears' habitat in a snow-covered wilderness without vegetation dictates that they are mostly carnivorous and despite this they maintain a high degree of purity and divine connection. Their pure white colour indicates that they are highly evolved and are preparing for ascension at the end of their current lifetime.

Polar bears are very connected to the diamond-white light of Archangel Gabriel as are most animals who live in the snow. Archangel Gabriel pours light into their crown chakras and enables them to hold their link to their higher selves and also bring through the ninth-dimensional frequencies of the Christ Light. They are very affected by the great portal in the Arctic that radiates pure white Christ energy.

Because of their symbiotic relationship with water they also work with Archangel Joules, the angel of the oceans. They bring their high-frequency light into the waters of the Arctic and do their part to hold the energy high here while he bathes them in the cosmic love held within the waters.

When you think about, see or meditate on a polar bear you connect to Archangel Gabriel and his diamond-white flame. Through this he is able to link you to the Seraphim Seraphina and her Intergalactic schools, where beings from all over the universes come to train to become Intergalactic Masters. Completely unconsciously the polar bears are doing mighty cosmic service work and helping your ascension and the ascension of the planet.

VISUALIZATION TO WORK WITH THE BEAR KINGDOM

1. Find a place where you can be quiet and undisturbed.

2. Light a candle if you wish and dedicate it to the higher selves of the magnificent bears.

3. Sense or see yourself in a beautiful, rugged place out in nature. There are snow-topped mountains in the distance and a wide, clear, fast-flowing stream rushes through the valley.

4. You sit quietly on a big flat stone in the river and enjoy the bright sunshine pouring all over you, and relaxing you. All is peaceful.

5. Archangel Uriel sits in his golden light beside you. You feel totally safe.

6. You notice a bear in the river, quietly fishing and playing all by itself. There is a pale golden light linking it to Archangel Jophiel and beyond to the love aspect of Orion.

7. Archangel Uriel's angels of peace sing over the bear and you sense its inner strength and harmony.

8. The bear looks up at you and a path of liquid gold forms between you. Golden shimmering love pours down on you. Bathe in this wondrous energetic gift and relax.

9. Thank the bear and Archangels Uriel and Jophiel.

10. You are finding yourself wrapped in a very warm coat, hat and boots in a pure white world.

11. A polar bear is sitting on an ice floe, calmly watching the melted water round him.

12. You are aware that the shimmering diamond-white light above him is Archangel Gabriel, and all at once you feel his wondrous pure soft wings around you. Your heart feels warm and safe!

13. Then suddenly a vast ice-white Ascension Flame appears in front of you and the wondrous Seraphim Seraphina smiles at you from the centre of it.

14. When she touches you, you feel her blazing energy going through you. You are expanding.

15. New choices are now available to you. Relax and know that your connection with Seraphina through the polar bear has shifted something amazing within you.

16. Thank Seraphina and the polar bear. Return to where you started and open your eyes.

Chapter 5

Beavers

Message from the Beavers
Work tirelessly towards your vision and remember to do so with love. And know that clear, running water will keep your heart and mind pure. Then you can connect more easily with the angels.

Beavers originate from Lakumay, the ascended aspect of Sirius. They are mostly nocturnal rodents who spend a great deal of their time in water. Like all water-based animals they have pure clear auras and their connection to Hollow Earth, the seventh-dimensional chakra in the centre of the Earth, is through Archangel Joules.

Their main soul mission is to keep the waters pure and clean as well as to build and maintain the ecosystem of the waterways in which they live. For thousands of years they have helped to keep their local habitats pure and clean by building pools; in doing so they clear mud and weeds. Their work also creates wetlands, thus forming an ecosystem that supports many other species of animal in an uncontaminated environment.

They are noted for their industry and for their ability to fell trees in order to build dams and their homes, which are called lodges. A beaver colony works together to construct a dam in order to create still deep water. Their building techniques are very skilled. They create a frame of upright poles and then they weave branches through it. Finally, they solidify it with mud and weeds until it forms a waterproof dam. They bring this building knowledge with them from Sirius, and when humans were starting to evolve, beavers demonstrated to them how to build their homes.

The entrances to their lodges are underwater so they cleverly have two dens inside. The first is to dry their fur in. The second is their dry living quarters. Here the adults may live with several of their babies and their older siblings.

Beavers are also learning and teaching about family life within a unit headed by a monogamous pair. The male and female mate for life. Only if their partner dies will a beaver find another mate. They are discovering masculine-feminine balance. Both raise the kits together. Both mark their territory and defend it. As nature decrees the mother is the primary carer in the first month after their babies are born while the father protects the territory.

There are two types of beaver, the Eurasian beavers and the North American ones. They have physical differences and are genetically incompatible. However, they incarnate with the same spiritual and soul purpose.

With their webbed feet beavers can swim fast and smoothly. Their wide flat tail enables them to carry their young if they wish to. They have poor vision for they do not need it as they have a very keen sense of hearing, smell and touch.

For thousands of years, humans have trapped beavers. As a result of such persecution these beautiful animals are wary of people but they demonstrate fifth-dimensional open heart-centres and an evolved way of perceiving the world from a higher perspective. They show us it is possible to live in joy and happiness whatever the circumstances. Like all species their lives are dedicated to survival but the beavers are very much focused on acting for the highest good.

VISUALIZATION TO UNDERSTAND THE WORLD OF BEAVERS

1. Find a place where you can be quiet and undisturbed.

2. Light a candle and dedicate it to understanding the world of beavers.

3. You are sitting peacefully at the edge of a waterway.

4. A magnificent beaver with a lovely sleek shiny coat appears beside you.

5. Stroke its thick, luxurious coat. Then have a sense of a similar coat around you.

6. Have a feeling that your body is becoming smaller. Your teeth are growing and you have whiskers, tiny ears and a broad, flat tail. You have become a beaver.

7. Your beaver companion dives into the pool and you dive freely, happily after him, using your webbed hindfeet to thrust powerfully forward through the water. You play and slap the water with your tail. See the trees you have felled to make a dam. Take your time to enjoy this.

8. Now you slip through an underground hole into your lodge, where you shake yourself and dry off.

9. And now you move with your new companion into the inner chamber and join your family. You feel happy and confident and relaxed.

10. At last you slip out of the lodge and return to the edge of the pool.

11. Thank the beavers for this experience and find yourself back in your human body.

Chapter 6

~

Camels

Message from the Camels

Resources are finite but there is enough for everyone when shared with wisdom and common sense. Together we can make our planet into a beautiful paradise again.

Camels have two humps and dromedaries have one. These animals are very ancient beings who originally came to Earth into North America, Canada and the Arctic some 45 million years ago. At that time, they were enormous, much bigger than the camels we know now, and without the humps. About four million years ago they migrated across the Bering Straits to Asia and further south, which is where they are mostly found now. This is why we always associate them with Asia, Africa and even parts of Australia. In those ancient times they were third-dimensional.

Concurrent with the Age of Atlantis the Intergalactic Council was overseeing other experiments on Earth, including one in Africa and one in Asia. As with the challenge of Atlantis these trials were designed to find the best way for spirits to enter a body and maintain their divine connections. The oversoul of the camels offered to take part in these divine tasks in order to serve and to learn. Those who had ascended to Lakumay, the higher aspect of Sirius, and were fifth-dimensional, agreed to incarnate in Asia and Africa in the camel bodies we recognize now.

So these very wise, knowing and intelligent animals incarnated in smaller bodies with their fatty humps, to freely offer their milk and skins and their strength and fortitude to the people of those regions. In exchange they would learn and teach about serving humanity with patience and endurance. It takes mighty beings to agree to endure extremes of heat and cold and to be long-distance runners at consistent speeds of 25mph, while storing food and water on their backs, working for those most exacting and demanding of taskmasters, human beings. They do this to develop qualities of humility, patience and forbearance that they can take back in their energy fields to Lakumay. They are also testing their powers of physical endurance.

When Atlantis fell the whole world was affected, much of it thrown into chaos. The camels, however, maintained their fifth-dimensional level despite all that was happening around them.

And now they are learning about balance and to transform negativity into light. One minute they carry heavy loads for mile after mile across inhospitable deserts, where they have time and space to contemplate, then they are in the centre of chaotic, noisy, often crowded places where they must hold their energy steady while they absorb and transmute the low frequencies around them. They are learning to balance. Archangel Jophiel assists them with this but nevertheless it is no wonder they have a reputation for being bad-tempered sometimes.

A third lesson they are demonstrating to us is to use resources wisely. They must carry their food and drink and may not have the opportunity to replenish their supply for some time. They soon learn to conserve what they have and use it with discrimination. This is a particularly important concept for people to grasp at this time.

The only occasion I rode on a camel, many years ago on a holiday in Africa, I was decidedly nervous of its imperious, even malicious, look and scruffy appearance. Furthermore, it looked huge. When it rose, with me on its back, and swayed alarmingly as it walked, I was positively scared. I felt mightily relieved when my ride was over. That was before I was on my spiritual path and I knew nothing about angels. I'm ashamed to say I don't even remember thanking that camel for its service.

The camels remained in Asia, Africa and the Middle East because this was where their service work was most needed. When enough people in these areas have become fifth-dimensional the camels will pass information to them to help them through the transition period to the new Golden Age starting in 2032. They will do this in two ways – firstly, as more humans become telepathically receptive, the camels will pour downloads directly into their minds. Secondly, when humans are ready the sacred geometric blueprint of the camels will overlay that of humans who are ready and this will trigger our own innate knowledge and wisdom.

The blueprint carried by the camels contains much sacred knowledge from Sirius. As these beasts walk across the deserts they pass this information and golden light into the ley lines. Part of their service work is to maintain the dragon lines, the fifth-dimensional ley lines of the planet. So they are helping to maintain the grids for us all.

Angels and Masters Who Work with Camels

Like all animals, camels have two guardian angels who look after them and support their missions. When they are dispirited it is the task of their angels to encourage them and remind them of the undertaking their soul accepted. Their guardian angels also merge with the angels of their riders so that many beings of light accompany them on their journeys. These angels help to lighten their load and ease the hardship they endure as well as to communicate with those who ride on them or walk with them.

Naturally the angel of animals, Archangel Fhelyai, remains with them constantly and brings them comfort as well as guidance.

Archangel Jophiel, the yellow angel of wisdom, is in charge of the development of the whole of Asia, and he oversees the lives of these animals, for the knowledge they hold is integral to the unfoldment of Asia in divine right order.

El Morya was a High Priest in Atlantis and has worked consistently to develop knowledge and spiritual understanding in this part of the world. He now works closely with camels even though they were not part of the experiment of Atlantis.

Apollo was also a High Priest in Atlantis and he led his tribe to Mesopotamia after the Fall of Atlantis, bringing the wisdom of his tribe to this place. He particularly understood about water and its cosmic properties, and the art of irrigation. Camels remember the time when the deserts were green and fertile and how this was maintained. Because they earned the right to receive it, a great deal of this information was subsequently encoded into these animals so that they can pass it to those who are ready at the appropriate time.

The Future

As we move towards the new Golden Age in 2032, two things will happen. First, the climate will become more extreme, so that information about water conservation and irrigation will be essential and, secondly, humanity will raise its frequency to the fifth dimension, so we will be receptive to the knowledge and wisdom the camels offer.

In 2012 the 33 cosmic portals around the planet started to open, pouring out Christ Light and much higher knowledge encoded within sacred geometric shapes. With the assistance of their guardian angels these amazing animals are holding this light within their auric fields as they wait patiently for us to be ready.

Now I want to take you into a visualization to help you connect with the extraordinary knowledge and wisdom of the camel kingdom. When I meditated on this I learned that I could not merge with the energy of the camel's higher self. The Archangels Jophiel and Fhelyai offered to place the camel's higher self and mine in a cocoon together. The cocoon is made of their joint energy and when we were within it we could exchange light, which holds spiritual information and knowledge, at a soul level. This is then held in our human energy fields until we are ready to use it for the benefit of the world.

The archangels hope that if enough people practise this meditation it will accelerate the raising of the frequency of the planet.

VISUALIZATION TO CONNECT WITH AND HELP THE CAMELS

1. Find a space where you can be quiet and undisturbed.
2. Light a candle if you wish to.
3. Call in Archangel Fhelyai, the magnificent yellow angel of animals, and feel his energy surround you.
4. Call in Archangel Jophiel and feel his pale crystal-yellow light pouring through you.

5. The archangel energy is raising your frequency and you find yourself rising up through the dimensions to a place in Lakumay, where everything is shimmering with beautiful light.

6. The higher self of a representative of the camel kingdom is approaching you in its awesome light.

7. Sit quietly with this being and feel the love from your heart connecting with its heart energy.

8. Archangels Fhelyai and Jophiel are merging their extraordinary yellow shimmering light to form a sunshine-yellow cocoon around you both.

9. Rest and relax here, keeping your mind as still as possible. As you do this your souls are connecting and illuminating each other.

10. When the cocoon lifts, thank the camel's higher self as it slowly withdraws from your sight.

11. Allow Archangels Fhelyai and Jophiel to conduct you lovingly back to where you started.

12. Thank them and keep your heart open to the camels who are serving our planet.

Chapter 7
~

Cats

Message from the Cats

*We see and know everything for we are enlightened
beings. We watch over your homes and the planet
and keep the frequency high. When we are snoozing
in the sun we may be doing important service
work. You too often do spiritual work when you
are relaxing, so learn from us and rest more.*

All cats originate from Orion, the constellation of enlightenment
and wisdom, and they teach and demonstrate many qualities
of enlightenment to us. Orion has ascended, so all beings from
here are fifth-dimensional. Knowledge is of no use unless you
know how to apply it wisely, and all creatures who come from
Orion are able to take information and use it with wisdom.

Cats spread wisdom by their very presence and their auras
trigger our own innate wisdom. These animals also bring
qualities of enlightenment to Earth. They spread peace and
healing and they show us how to relax deeply to a cellular level
and then move with wonderfully fluid movements.

Cats are healers and work with Archangel Raphael. Since the
Cosmic Moment in 2012 – an instant at 11.11 on 21 December

2012 that marked the end of the civilization of Atlantis, during which Source energy touched the heart of every sentient being throughout the universes and set ascension of all in progress – they have connected to Archangel Mariel, who brings higher soul healing through them in an attempt to raise the frequency of the planet more quickly.

All cats, whether small domestic ones or huge lions and tigers, are independent beings, relaxed when it is appropriate to be so. They do not need humans but are here to serve us.

Domestic Cats

The domestic cats who arrived in the golden era of Atlantis took on the service role of keeping the homes or temples in which they lived clear of lower energies. At that time every home or building had a resident cat and they were very much respected. All the cats of this era were black. This signified the divine feminine, the mysterious and psychic.

When the golden high-frequency energy of Atlantis started to devolve, the first thing that the Magi did was send to Orion for more cats to try to hold the frequency. Unfortunately, it was too late.

Then and now domestic cats help people to interpret and understand situations with the eyes of wisdom. This is done subtly and we humans have no idea how much help we are receiving from our feline friends.

Cats are very psychic. They know exactly what is happening and where people are at all times. Any cat owner (though I use the word 'owner' lightly) knows this.

As I drove into my garage after being away from home for ten weeks I was not surprised that my little grey moggy appeared and was standing by the driver's door to greet me as I stepped out of the car.

When cats purr they are usually signalling that they are contented and happy or they may be saying they are friendly. Cats may purr to soothe you or a potential enemy.

However, they may also purr to reassure and calm themselves. When they purr, endorphins are released which can help in pain management. It is fascinating that a cat purrs at 25–150Hz, which is also the frequency that is beneficial in physical healing and bone mending. So your cat may be self-healing or even transmitting that healing to you.

Wild Cats

Wild cats are not connected to humans and their service work is to the planet and other animals. They help to look after the area in which they live and keep it clear of unwanted energies.

Big Cats

The big cats watch over our planet and protect it from unwanted entities or negative energies approaching Earth. They help to keep us in alignment with other planets and stars in the universe. They are also healers.

There were no big cats in the golden era of Atlantis. The energy was so harmonious that small cats could do what was needed. The big cats on Earth at that time were part of another experiment.

The Pharaohs used big cats to bolster their power because the frequency was considerably lower by then.

Black Panther

Black panthers, pumas, leopards, cougars and jaguars with a black pigmentation are highly evolved fifth-dimensional beings and incarnate in service to humans, other animals and the planet.

They come from America, Latin America, Asia and Africa but many have escaped from zoos or private collections, so are now found in Europe and other continents. The escapes are orchestrated by the angels as part of a spiritual plan to help humanity. They are extremely elusive so are almost impossible to pinpoint and recapture.

When you need to wake up spiritually a black panther may appear as your wake-up call. These animals would never physically hurt you – they are on a spiritual mission when you see them. However, if a black panther is sent to wake you up and you resist the process by running away, you could hurt yourself as you do so.

The son of a friend of mine was an alcoholic. He was well off his life path and needed a big nudge from spirit. He was taking his young dog for a walk by a canal late one evening when he heard a rustle in the bushes by the path. He swung his torch towards the sound and to his horror the beam picked up two huge luminous cat's eyes. Instantly he jumped for safety into the canal, which was being dredged. He found himself completely stuck in mud, unable to move – an exact analogy for his life situation.

By good fortune he was holding his mobile, though his wife took some persuasion to believe it was not a hoax. She was more worried about their precious puppy than about him. Eventually he was rescued and the little dog was found very sensibly cowering under the car. The following day the big cat paw prints were still visible but, although the police cordoned off the area, it was never found. The panther was probably on another mission far away.

The man recognized that his life was metaphorically stuck in the mud. He was not aware that the black panther had appeared to him to give him a wake-up call. As a result of that encounter he almost had a breakdown, which then turned into a breakthrough in his life as he joined a twelve-step programme. A year later, because he stopped drinking, he saved his faltering marriage and found a job that satisfied his soul.

Leopards

These are cats of great grace, agility and beauty. They also demonstrate awesome strength.

In the great plan, each type of cat has been developing slightly different qualities and abilities to take back to Orion.

The leopard is the most beautiful and widespread of all big cats. While all cats can climb, the leopard has developed this ability more than any other of the species. It can carry prey twice its own weight up a tree.

Cheetahs

Cheetahs have particularly developed their speed. They are the world's fastest land mammal and can run at speeds of up to 70 miles an hour and they can cover up to eight metres in one stride!

Cheetahs do not roar like the other big cats. They purr. This loud purr spreads healing and contentment as well as soothing cheetah kittens.

Lions

Lions are known as the king of beasts and are sometimes depicted with a crown on their heads, symbolizing that their crown chakras are open to the higher energies of the universe. They work with Archangel Jophiel who is in charge of the crown chakra and helps to make their stellar connections.

As with all other cats their soul mission is to keep the frequency in their areas high. Lions (and tigers) in particular watch over Earth and at the same time heal and protect our planet.

An adult lion has a very well-developed throat chakra and its roar can be heard up to five miles away. Its roar is not just about proclaiming its territory and telling stray members of the pride where to meet it. The terrifying roar is usually emitted at night when the sound can travel further in the atmospherics. It goes out into space, warning and frightening away negative entities that are approaching us with lower intent. At the same time the roar contains healing vibrations that go into the ground itself.

Lions are the only cats that live in groups. A pride is a family group of lionesses with one lion. Spiritually they are now learning about family life as they develop new aspects of their feminine nature.

The Great Zimbabwe is sometimes called the resting place of the lions. This is one of the four two-way inter-dimensional portals on the planet.

Tigers

These magnificent, totally psychic animals incarnate with a vital soul mission and they do this with love in their hearts for humanity and the planet – to watch out for lower entities or energies approaching the planet and raise the energy around them with the intention of transmuting them. Their roars are designed to warn other creatures off their territory and also to send a verbal warning out into space to any entities thinking of attacking Earth, especially these days when our planetary aura is weak.

Their stripes are unique, like human fingerprints, and no two animals have the same pattern.

Most cats dislike and avoid water. However, it is part of the tigers' mission to develop a relationship with water and understand it. In pursuance of this goal they have come to love water and enjoy swimming and catching fish. They will take their understandings back to the Masters of Orion and will carry the universal love held in water in their energy fields.

Despite the fact that there are very few of them left, with open-hearted generosity they do their very best to look after all of us on the planet.

The Tiger Temple

In 2008 I went on holiday to Thailand with my friend Rosemary. The day before we flew her son showed her a video of the tigers who had been rescued and cared for by the monks at the Tiger Temple. We were determined to go and see them.

We were told that at the Tiger Temple the monks practise deep meditation and have a wildlife sanctuary, where injured animals are treated with love and compassion and allowed to roam freely in the grounds. Several tiger cubs, whose mothers had been killed by poachers, were brought to them and they were cared for so that they all survived, flourished and grew.

Our first glimpse was of three fluffy four-week-old cubs playing in the sand with their handlers. Other tigers lay nonchalantly around and we were warned not to walk in front of them but we could touch them from behind. Before we met the big tigers and walked down to the canyon with them, they were sprayed with water to cool them down.

I walked beside the oldest tiger – a huge male. One of my hands was firmly on his back and I could feel his strength and smell his wet fur. Seven tigers were brought down to the canyon where they were soon fast asleep in the baking sun.

Big cats are watchers of the Earth just as domestic ones protect a home from entities. As I sat on the ground by the big tiger and cradled his magnificent head on my lap, I telepathically thanked him for his service in looking after our planet. He clearly received the message for suddenly he raised his head and looked round, as if seeking the source of the communication. This alarmed the monks, who were with me in an instant, pulling the tiger off me and settling him down again! But I felt thrilled.

Later my spirit guide, Kumeka, said that the tiger had indeed received the message I sent him and was greatly heartened by it. He said I had been sent there to give the tiger hope.

Since then I have heard and read differing and controversial reports about what happens at the tiger sanctuary, so all I can do is share my experience and offer this prayer.

Prayer for the Tigers, Lions and All Big Cats

Beloved Source and Archangel Fhelyai, angel of animals,

From the depth of my heart I ask you to fill the hearts of all humans with love and respect for the tigers, lions and all big cats and touch the minds of all humans with understanding and intention to help them.

Please pass the thanks of humanity to these beautiful animals who watch over our planet and help to hold the frequency as high as possible. Fill them with hope.

Thank you.

Chapter 8

~

Cows

Message from the Cows

We love Earth and humanity and are very happy to serve by offering our milk. However, we do expect gratitude and care in exchange, for this balances the karma between us.

Cows originate from Lakumay, the ascended aspect of Sirius. They were one of the first service animals to come to Earth in the golden era of Atlantis to offer their milk to humanity. At that time their milk was perfectly attuned to the needs of humans because the grass and wild flowers that they consumed were at a much higher frequency than they are now. The water was pure and blessed too. The people did not eat meat so they greatly benefited from the milk. As fifth-dimensional beings from Lakumay, cows bring in the unconditional love and divine feminine light of the Gold Ray of Christ and pass it on through their milk.

Cows demonstrate comfortable, motherly, nurturing and giving qualities. They are warm and solid, gentle and earthed. They originally incarnated to develop these stable, reliable aspects of their nature and have done so beautifully. They are the ultimate feminine, benevolent, loving animal. And the

Great Spiritual Mother, the Universal Angel, Mary, constantly holds and bathes them in her loving light.

Bulls are tough and steady. They demonstrate masculine power and protection. Together they offer a perfect balance of masculine and feminine energy.

In the golden era of Atlantis cows and bulls were considered part of the family. They were loved and cared for. The people enjoyed and gave thanks for the rich milk of the cows and every animal was appreciated as an individual. They gave and received love in equal measure.

As the world became third-dimensional cows were treated as commodities and suffered intolerably. They were fed inappropriate food and expected to perform to their milk quotas or die. Their calves were killed and eaten. This greatly stressed the cows and angered the bulls.

Stressed people and animals are open to illness. Eventually the herds suffered from mad cow disease and thousands were slaughtered. At last humans began to realize that we need them more than they need us.

At this time the highly evolved oversoul of the domestic cattle was seriously discussing with the Intergalactic Council whether they should withdraw from Earth and continue to experience on another planet of their choice. This would have created a terrible hole in the plan for Earth and also much karma for humanity and this planet that the cows truly love in their hearts.

Surrender is a feminine quality and the cows demonstrated it when they allowed themselves to be sacrificed and burned in their hundreds on blazing funeral fires. The flames helped to transmute and purify the energy of pain, suffering and disrespect that had been inflicted on them for thousands of years. Unbelievably, humanity has not learned its lesson and is still mistreating these beautiful animals.

So many prayers were sent out for the cows then and since that great portals of light were created and Archangel Fhelyai's angels poured into the planet to help them. Archangel Zadkiel filled these portals with his Gold and Silver Violet Flame to transmute and heal. Archangels Raphael and Gabriel sent thousands of angels to accompany to the other side each cow that died in this way. The valiant souls of these animals were received back in Lakumay with glorious ceremony and universal greetings.

However, thankfully for Earth the oversoul of the cows listened to the arguments of the Intergalactic Council. Because we were entering the 20-year period of transition to the fifth dimension, when the entire planet is rising in frequency, the cattle kingdom decided to grace us with their presence for a while longer.

Between 2012 and 2032 all animals, humans and the planet itself are on a journey to the fifth dimension. When the world lives in that advanced state of consciousness cows and bulls will be treated with respect and gratitude once more. Then they will truly be able to give and receive with love. They will at last enjoy being here to continue their spiritual growth and learning as they originally anticipated.

Holy Cows

The mighty Hindu god or great master Krishna is depicted as a cowherd. His name Bala Gopala means 'the child who protects the cows'. Another of his names, Govinda, means 'one who brings satisfaction to the cows'. In the Hindu faith the cow is considered as the bountiful mother because her milk nurtures the people and every part of her is utilized in some useful way. She is revered and considered to be holy. Where this belief is genuinely and honestly held the energy helps to raise the frequency of cows worldwide. It has sustained them.

VISUALIZATION BACK IN TIME TO CONNECT WITH COWS

1. Find a place where you feel comfortable and undisturbed.

2. Light a candle if possible to raise the frequency.

3. Close your eyes and allow your eyelids to feel heavy, very heavy, as you breathe more deeply.

4. A shimmering golden bridge is appearing in front of you.

5. You know this is a gateway to the incredible era of Golden Atlantis.

6. Cross the bridge knowing you are being guided and held by the angels.

7. As you reach the end of the bridge you can see Golden Atlantis ahead of you. Everything is shimmering with a golden aura – the trees, the grass, the round houses that are clustered together, the flowing water, the birds, everything.

8. In wonder and delight you step onto the land and immediately feel welcome and happy.

9. As you approach one of the round houses you can hear beautiful music, joy-filled laughter and the tinkle of water flowing.

10. The garden is a colourful pasture blooming with perfumed wild flowers.

11. A family is playing in the sunshine. Father and mother, three children and three dogs are splashing in a pure clear pool. They are watched by their black cat, a horse, a cow, a sheep and a goat, who are resting under a tree together.

12. The family call you to join them and you swim in the water with them.

13. Then the contented cow wanders up to you and looks at you with liquid brown eyes full of love.

14. You stroke it and wonder at her sparkling golden aura.

15. She tells you telepathically that she serves the family with love, offering them rich milk for cheese and butter. In return they give her shelter, beautiful pastures and loving gratitude.

16. Everyone is contented and they all love being on Earth.

17. The mother politely asks the cow if she may take some milk for you and the cow graciously agrees.

18. The mother draws the milk and offers it to you in a cup. This milk is perfectly calibrated for a fifth-dimensional vibration and you receive it with thanks.

19. As you drink the fifth-dimensional elixir you feel every cell of your body light up.

20. You walk back across the bridge with a deep connection to the cow kingdom. This light and love is now in your aura.

21. When you see a cow in future the energy in your aura will remind them of who they truly are. You will make a difference.

Chapter 9

~

Deer

Message from the Deer

When you see a deer you are asked to trust the universe or trust your own intuition. Look within and strengthen your inner processes. We will radiate to you the courage, strength, grace and harmony that you need. So stand in your wisdom and power.

Deer in all their different forms have incarnated from Lakumay, the ascended aspect of Sirius, to learn and teach about trust. The gentle doe appears to be nervous and ready to run at the slightest sign of disturbance. She tests the energies, sniffing the air, and is constantly watchful, working with her third eye open.

However, as my little dog, Venus, found out, the doe is as fierce as a tiger if her fawn is threatened. Venus was a deer-chaser and there were many deer in our forest. One day she raced off intent on pursuit. I heard the crashing of undergrowth followed by loud squealing and thought it was Venus vocalizing the thrill of the chase. A few seconds later my dog shot out of the bracken, chased by a very angry deer. Venus ran to my side and the deer stood glaring at us and stamping until we walked quietly away. She must have had a fawn hidden nearby.

Anyway, Venus learned that lesson. She has never chased a deer since.

Between them the doe and stag balance the masculine and feminine energies. The stag is strong, courageous, dignified and proud. He is often considered to represent strength, and his fabulous antlers symbolize dominance and power. He is grounded in his power.

Stags grow antlers in the spring and this denotes birth and renewal. They fall off in the winter and this signifies death, endings, introspection or loss. So if you see a stag it can indicate a change in direction or a new start in some aspect of your life. It also suggests that you have the confidence and inner power to do so. Stags are connected to Archangel Michael, who works through these animals to touch people and give them the strength to do what they need to do. Archangel Michael also connects to humans through stags to impress on them to look after those weaker than themselves.

Does are soft, loving and harmonious (unless her fawn is threatened). They also represent innocence. They are graceful and delicate. People are often transfixed by the sight of a doe with her beauty and grace. Archangel Michael and his twin flame Archangel Faith are often seen with a herd of deer. Archangel Michael gives them strength while Archangel Faith bolsters their trust levels.

While their soul mission is to learn and teach about beauty, grace and trust in the universe, their service mission is to eat fresh grasses and leaves in order to stimulate new growth.

They are also learning and teaching about their brand of family life, where the male tends to lead a solitary existence while the females bring up the fawns. The doe learns about cooperation and working together as a group.

Like many evolved animals they take any opportunity they can to raise the frequency of humanity. In my book, *Venus, the Diary of a Puppy and her Angel*, I tell the story of a stag who escaped from a nearby deer farm and decided to live in a plantation of newly planted conifers. He graced his little patch in the sunshine every day and the news of his presence was soon flying everywhere. People poured in from miles around to catch a glimpse of him. At first he was radiating out an energy to help people to have trust in the universe. Then after a few days, the message he was sending out changed to one of community togetherness. His presence was inspiring people to connect and talk to each other. Archangel Michael was passing this energy through his throat chakra to us all.

Like all animals who incarnate from Lakumay, the deer are downloading into the auras of those who are ready to receive knowledge about the spiritual technology of the future as well as sacred geometry. The angels sing over them as they do this to enable the keys and codes to be transferred more easily.

You can ask the angels to help any animal. I once passed a herd of deer quietly grazing. I felt impressed to ask Archangel Fhelyai, the angel of animals, to send one of his angels to each one of the animals. Instantly I saw a yellow light appear by one, and then another and quickly they were all lit up with yellow lights. It really was beautiful. Whether you can see or sense the lights or not, when you ask for angelic help, this automatically happens.

Visualization to Connect with the Deer

1. Find a place where you feel relaxed and can be undisturbed.
2. Light a candle if you can, then close your eyes and breathe comfortably.
3. When your eyelids feel really heavy imagine you can hear the dawn chorus.

4. Visualize yourself at the top of a verdant wild-flower-filled hillside. You may even smell the fragrance.

5. As a bright red-orange sun rises over the hilltop you see a magnificent regal stag silhouetted against the sun.

6. The light is glinting off his noble antlers.

7. A doe walks quietly in and stands beside him.

8. From his glowing heart the stag radiates qualities of majesty, strength, courage and power to you. Your aura fills with royal-blue light.

9. From her glowing heart the doe radiates qualities of gentleness, grace, love, harmony and innocence to you. Your aura fills with shimmering milky-white light.

10. Knowing you are safe, you look through their eyes into their souls. Sacred geometric symbols and codes of spiritual technology pour into your aura.

11. Feel your aura lighting up and blazing.

12. Now radiate this energy out into the world and know you are truly honouring the deer kingdom.

Chapter 10

Dogs

Message from the Dogs

*Your family is your foundation and contains the essence
of the lessons your soul has chosen for this lifetime.
True discipline and respect keeps it together and
enables you to walk your spiritual path with joy.*

All canines originate from Sirius. They are particularly here to explore and experience different forms of family structure.

Domestic Dogs

At the start of the fifth experiment of Atlantis, which birthed the Golden Age, there was much discussion between the Intergalactic Council and the Masters of Sirius. As a result, it was decided that dogs would be the most appropriate animal companions for those fifth-dimensional beings who were incarnating for the new experience. The Gold Ray of Christ is held in Sirius and all beings from there carry some of that golden unconditional love in their energy fields.

They realized that these new humans, who had never been to Earth before, would benefit from the unconditional love offered by dogs. It would also help to develop the people's heart centres if they had to look after the daily needs of an animal. And dogs would experience human families and learn to trust them. And so a new kind of dog, rather like lurchers, were given permission by Source to incarnate. It caused a frisson of excitement round the universe for no animal had lived truly intimately with humans or depended on them so completely as those who were now to be born.

These animals arrived in a unique way. Initially, a few young dogs apported from Sirius. Homes had been carefully prepared for them and, as they arrived, each one trotted off to its rightful family. These six families each had one child. They were expecting the young arrival. As soon as it appeared both the child and its parents immediately recognized it as their new family member.

The child bonded with its pet and was given the responsibility of feeding, grooming and walking with it. In return the dog accompanied the child to school as a friend and protector. These dogs represented a masculine energy in the household, where there was already a rabbit and a cat, who were feminine-orientated.

From the time that these original dogs reproduced, this system continued. Each puppy went to a child that was pre-arranged for it and was embraced and lovingly treated as part of the family. They played, frolicked and ran together, giving each other mutual companionship, love and joy.

When a new baby was born into a family, the parents automatically expected a puppy to arrive to accompany it on its journey through childhood. Indeed, when the child became an adult between the ages of thirteen and sixteen, it left home and the dog automatically passed over, having accomplished its mission.

A huge unbreakable bond had formed between the dog and human and thousands of years later this cord of love still draws human and animal together. We never lose our beloved pets. We always meet them again.

This state of happy co-living and loving lasted for 1,500 years until the energy started to degenerate and people slipped into a third-dimensional consciousness. As human egos started to take over, some people decided they had the right to interfere with the divine blueprints of the animals. They thought they could genetically alter and breed dogs for their own gratification. And so dogs became human playthings.

They were selectively modified to hunt other animals, to fight, to race, to retrieve or for many other uses. They became chattels and many were treated as such.

And still these beautiful creatures have incarnated again and again with their hearts open and hopeful.

In current times domestic dogs display a huge diversity of shapes, sizes, colours and temperaments. Their 'purpose' ranges from being a substitute baby to a gun dog to a ratter or a drug sniffer or a dozen other usages. They have been over-bred to such an extent that many have genetic defects, so that now humans are recognizing their folly, and the word mongrel to describe a non-thoroughbred dog is being superseded by the more acceptable term mixed breed – a dog who is less likely to have genetic defects.

However, their spiritual purpose on incarnation is still to give and receive love and to learn and teach about discipline.

Your dog loves you and may have been with you for many lifetimes. They 'choose' their owners in the same way that a baby is spiritually drawn to its parents. This means you can never get the wrong pet. Those important decisions are taken at a soul level.

If you feel you have known your dog before, you probably have.

Wolves

Wolves have always been regal canines, strong and independent. They incarnated to bring in the Gold Ray of Christ from Sirius, to spread it wherever they roamed and to learn about discipline and family life. They were also learning and teaching that it is more effective to work together than alone. The only thing they feared was humans.

When Atlantis fell the High Priest Imhotep led his tribe to the Americas and developed the Native American tribes. His people were more evolved than any previous 'humans' who had lived in these lands. The wolf faced his fear and started to trust people, and they, in turn, started to trust wolves. The ancient stories and paintings of the earliest peoples depicted wolf and human together. In some legends the wolf has healing powers and in one the wolf saved the people from a great flood.

Many Native Americans understood the humans' deep connection with the wolf.

Grey wolves lived over most of the United States. Unbelievably, in the 1960s they were declared to be vermin and were virtually exterminated. Only by hiding in the vast forests did any survive.

And when they were almost extinct humans declared them to be protected as an endangered species. The first pack of wild wolves crossed from Canada into Montana and became known as the Magic Pack.

At last their numbers are growing again and they can continue once more to develop their understanding of family life, with its very strict hierarchy and rules. Male and female wolves tend to be considered equal within the pack. They are holding the balance of the masculine and feminine energies from the golden era of Atlantis. Working together, they ensure each member of the family has a role to play and none are neglected.

Because wolves spread the Gold Ray of Christ wherever they roam Archangel Zariel looks after them as well as the angel of animals, Archangel Fhelyai.

They are spiritual teachers in their own right and spread much light to other members of the animal kingdom as well as to trees, plants and, if they will absorb it, to humans.

Foxes

Foxes originally incarnated into the Northern Hemisphere but, when humans introduced them to other parts of the world, they readily took the opportunity to spread in order to expand their learning experience.

One of the soul qualities they are developing is adaptability and they have proved that they can adjust amazingly to their environment. From foxes who climb trees to those who have developed huge ears so that they can dissipate heat in hot climes or Arctic foxes who grow thick pure-white fur in the snow they have proved themselves ready to cope with almost anything.

Foxes did not incarnate to live with humans but in some places they have been forced to change quickly. Where we have urbanized their natural habitats they have had to adapt. They have taken command of their energy fields and overcome their natural fear of us. Foxes have come to live amongst us in our towns and villages.

I remember the first time I visited my daughter in her new home in urban Surrey in the late 1990s. To my shock there were six foxes in the communal covered parking area. When I approached Lauren's front door a large vixen was lolling on the doorstep. It rose and slipped away as I approached.

When I mentioned this, that to me it was an extraordinary phenomenon, my daughter just shrugged and said they were always there but they didn't bother anyone. Twenty years later it is commonplace.

Like all the canine species foxes are learning and teaching about family life and discipline. Unlike wolves they are usually solitary or live in small family groups. They have a lot to teach us humans. Until I had my beloved dog, Venus, foxes were a common sight in my garden.

I was sitting on the patio one day when a vixen walked through the hedge followed by three cubs. They padded silently along, then she turned her head and looked at them, evidently giving them an instruction. Without a murmur all three spun round and trotted back the way they had come.

Remembering my own three robustly independent and argumentative children, I was awed by their instant obedience and absolute faith in their mother's instincts and discipline.

Once there were two vixens who gave birth to three cubs between them at almost the same time in a neighbouring garden. They formed a crèche, and one mother would look after the three cubs and often play with them on my lawn. Not only was it a joyful sight to watch the little ones playing under the watchful eye of mother or auntie, it demonstrates huge amounts of trust to allow your offspring to be looked after by another.

On several other occasions I have been sitting on the lawn while a fox has been sunbathing or gnawing a bone, or behaving in a dog-like fashion, just a metre or so away from me.

Now that I have a very territorial little dog, foxes hurry through my garden and I only see the whisk of a tail.

Like all animals who love to dig, foxes are connected to the element of earth and to Lady Gaia. When they dig a den or lair they bring the Christ Light right into the land itself.

Many people chase foxes away because they fear they carry a disease like mange or may even be rabid. And indeed they may be, for foxes have been stressed for centuries, ever since humans decided that they were good sport, and are vulnerable to disease. It is at least a mark of the rising consciousness of humanity that fox-hunting has been banned in the UK.

Others chase foxes away because they kill their fowl or the birds they have reared in order that they can enjoy the sport of shooting them themselves.

Dingos and Feral Dogs

The Australian dingo has descended from domestic dogs who became feral over many generations. They can still interbreed with domestic dogs.

There are many feral dogs throughout the world who have decided that they would rather fend for themselves than trust humans to look after them. They have never had contact with humans.

Spiritually, this is rather like a young person who decides to leave their family and emigrate to seek a new life. They are developing qualities of independence, resourcefulness, courage, adventure and adaptability amongst others.

Often they create their own packs, like wolves, and resurrect their original spiritual intention of learning and teaching about family life.

Usually the males leave the pack to seek a mate but in some African wild-dog packs the dog kingdom is trying a different experiment. The males stay with their birth family and the females leave in a group when they are old enough and seek out males to form a new pack.

Archangel Fhelyai, the angel of animals, oversees this and helps them to integrate their new understandings to take back to Sirius when they pass over.

Jackals and Coyotes

Jackals are wild dogs who live in Africa, Europe and parts of Asia. They can either hunt alone or in packs but sometimes they form small groups. Coyotes live in North America and are the counterpart of jackals. They are both predators who have overcome their deepest fear of humans and will take livestock or scavenge for garbage.

Many years ago I was holidaying in the USA with my family. In those days we were meat-eaters and were barbecuing thick steaks for dinner. In a flash a coyote ran past us, grabbed the meat off the grill and vanished. We could hardly believe our eyes and were left famished but in awe of the animal's courage and daring. I hope she fed her hungry family well!

Spiritually, our human take-over of the planet has forced jackals and coyotes to adapt to the possibilities around them. Their main spiritual purpose, however, is still to learn and teach about family life and to spread the energies of transcendent love that are held in their energy fields.

VISUALIZATION TO MAKE A BALL OF ENERGY FOR THE DOGS

1. Find a place where you can be quiet and undisturbed.

2. Breathing comfortably, call in the Gold Ray of Christ for your total protection and feel the golden energy streaming down over you.

3. Then breathe in a big breath. On the outbreath imagine yellow light flowing from your heart and forming a ball in front of you.

4. Continue to send out yellow light with your next few outbreaths, making the energy ball bigger.

5. When you have a big bright sunshine-yellow ball in front of you call in Archangel Fhelyai, the angel of animals, to help you. See or sense him standing by you.

6. Call in any dog or type of dog you wish and let them bathe in the ball of yellow light.

7. As they relax in the huge energy ball be aware of Archangel Fhelyai giving them what they need. This may be healing, relaxation, confidence, strength or any other quality.

8. See the dog emerge looking happy, healthy and free.

9. Thank Archangel Fhelyai and open your eyes knowing you have made a difference.

Chapter 11

Elephants

Message from the Elephants

*We represent cosmic abundance and when you are
ready to receive this into your life, we will be allowed
to live in peace. So bring true abundance into your
consciousness if you really want to help us.*

Five million years after the extinction of the dinosaurs, prehistoric elephants were some of the largest mammals on Earth. With their vast curved, ungainly tusks they were very different from the current much smaller African and Asian elephants who are, nevertheless, still the largest creatures on land.

Elephants were not part of Atlantis but when the first experiment was set up in that continent there were concurrent ones taking place in Africa and Asia. At that time elephants in the form that we now know them incarnated in fifth-dimensional bodies in both of these continents. They come from Lakumay, the ascended aspect of Sirius, and carry a fifth-dimensional blueprint for family life within a perfect matriarchal society.

These patient, gentle and wise animals incarnated to learn about family life and structure and to demonstrate it to humans.

They soon learned that the loving, caring, devoted qualities of the divine feminine are necessary when bringing up offspring and so mothers were revered and became central to family life. They were strong, patient and dominant. Bulls were protectors but kept away from the nucleus of the family.

Elephants also learned that joyous innocent fun kept their frequency high and maintained the cohesion of the group. Mothers and children love to play in mud and to squirt each other with water. Water was especially important as they recognized that it contains cosmic qualities and when kept at a fifth-dimensional frequency helps to dissolve any lower frequencies that might affect them.

Elephants are highly intelligent and also sensitive. They have emotions and feelings that can be hurt. I remember staying in a safari lodge in South Africa. A ranger humiliated one of the elephants in front of a group of visitors by chasing it out of the hotel and laughing at it. The man was being very macho, waving his stick, and the elephant literally ran away with its tail between its legs. But it did not forget. The rangers lived in huts in the grounds and the elephant returned during the night and pulled out all the water pipes from that man's hut; no one else's. That animal knew exactly where the bully lived. And it was a quick return of karma.

Elephants used to wander into the lodge and one morning I found a huge dump on the little patio outside my room. I wonder what message that pachyderm was bringing to me? It was certainly trying to draw my attention to its presence.

The oversoul of the elephants is very aware of its mission to teach about family life. Some years ago a group of young male elephants was creating havoc. They were going about in a teenage gang uprooting trees, fighting and behaving like elephant thugs. Impressed by Archangel Michael, the park rangers imported a strong dominant male bull, who wouldn't stand any nonsense. Immediately the laddish teenagers settled down. They grew up and behaved respectfully towards the big bull. There was no more trouble, and furthermore they all seemed much happier with a strong male role model to follow. This situation enabled the elephants to learn more about structured family life but it also demonstrated to humans how to deal effectively with gangs of youngsters – if they choose to follow the elephant example.

Because of their mission to demonstrate the message of happy family life elephants work with the great Universal Angel Mary. She acts as a loving advisor, whispering encouragement, hope and right action to them.

The Universal Angel Mary's twin flame is Archangel Raphael, the emerald-green angel who is in charge of the development of the third eye of all sentient beings. These great animals communicate with each other over several kilometres by infrasound, which is a much higher frequency than we use and is beyond our auditory range. In addition, they are very telepathic and tune in to psychic information via their trunk and third eye.

Archangel Raphael is also in charge of healing and abundance. Elephants are very connected to him and he heals through them. They leave a trail of his crystal-emerald healing light wherever they walk and this helps to raise the frequency of the land.

A nickname for elephants is Jumbo, meaning huge. It is no coincidence that the cosmic third eye chakra is Jupiter and its ascended aspect is Jumbay, meaning vast, expanded, higher perspective. When humans' third eye is ready to tune in to Jumbay, they can access a vast, higher, expanded, enlightened perspective on life. They can tune in to cosmic abundance, which includes all sorts of prosperity, love, happiness, success and a higher way of being. The elephants are able to do this all the time and part of their mission is to spread abundance consciousness.

Elephants are very connected to Earth. They root into the Earth Star chakra of the planet and work with Archangel Sandalphon, the black-and-white angel in charge of the Earth Star. He helps them to link their energy to the ley lines. For centuries they have lit up the third-dimensional lines as they walk their journeys. In addition, the geometric structure within their energy fields helps energetically to mend broken ley lines.

Since 2012 Archangel Metatron has been pouring gold light into the old ley-line structures and starting to build a crystalline web of light around the planet at a seventh-dimensional frequency. To help with this the elephants are tuning in to Lakumay and are facilitating the transfer of information from here directly into the new lines. They are helping to build the new spiritual communication system for the new Golden Age.

Elephants and the Pleiades

Elephants are also healers and work with the Angels of the Pleiades, spreading Source healing.

Elephants and Elementals

Elephants have pure innocent hearts, as do many of the great animals who walk the plains of Africa and Asia. The elementals gather round them and these vast evolved animals teach them and help to heal and protect them.

How to Help the Elephants

The situation on Earth has become so dire that elephants need a great deal of protection. Humans are a bridge between the angelic kingdoms and all on Earth. We have the power to make a difference. If enough people of goodwill prayed to Archangel Fhelyai, angel of animals, to help the elephants it would transform the current situation. And we need people to ask Archangel Fhelyai's angels to talk to the higher selves of poachers, ivory importers – anyone who buys ivory – and tourists to remind them of the importance of these majestic pachyderms. And also to explain that there are other ways to attract prosperity that earn no karma and positively benefit the world.

Prayer to Help the Elephants

Beloved Source, Archangels Fhelyai, Sandalphon, Mary and Raphael,

I open my fifth-dimensional heart to you and pray with the fire of my soul for protection of the elephants in the world.

I ask that you open the hearts of humanity to them, so that we treat them with love, honour and respect, and learn from them.

I also ask that you touch the collective mind of humanity and impress us all with a deep understanding of the importance and worth of the elephant kingdom and a desire to help them.

I ask that the energy of those who have harmed elephants is channelled into worthwhile pursuits and that a cloak of true abundance is placed over them for their highest good.

I ask that the elephant kingdom receives this energy of love.

So be it. It is done.

You can also use this prayer to ask for help for any animal that is being exploited.

Chapter 12

Giraffes

Message from the Giraffes

When you tune in to the giraffes you start to see life from a higher perspective. Bring more balance, grace and wisdom into your life. Add more courage, gentleness and calm. Then you will have learned the lesson we come to teach.

Giraffes incarnated in their current form as part of a divine experiment in Africa. This particular venture seeded some of the amazingly shaped animals that we now take for granted on that continent.

Giraffes originate from Orion, the constellation of light and wisdom, so they automatically carry in their energy fields some of the illumined light of that plane. They are overseen by the Masters and Angels of Orion, who watch over them with tender care.

These delightful fifth-dimensional creatures agreed to be enormously tall, with long spindly legs and a very long neck, so that they could fulfil their service mission of trimming the treetops. They can reach up and thin the leaves and pull out dead twigs to allow new growth. They are very tuned in to nature and the natural world.

These wise animals show qualities of gentleness, dignity and grace. Although they appear superficially to have more feminine characteristics they are very well balanced and able to protect themselves when necessary. Their kick is formidable and not to be underestimated. And they can gallop away from danger.

Giraffes are often depicted in children's books with a crown on their heads. This is because many artists often see unconsciously through the Veils of Illusion that separate the physical world from the higher spiritual dimensions. They are aware that the petals of the giraffes' crown chakras are open and can reach up into the universe for knowledge and wisdom. Archangel Jophiel, the archangel of wisdom, who is in charge of the development of the crown chakra, works with the giraffe kingdom. He helps them to keep this spiritual centre open and active so that they can stay connected with their birth planet of Orion and also with many other planets, stars and galaxies.

Masters and Angels of Orion also pour light, containing universal spiritual information and knowledge, through a ray of truth into the crown chakras of the giraffes.

While their service mission is to trim the trees, their soul mission is to channel the wisdom of Orion and spread it through their physical bodies into the Earth and into the ley lines of the planet.

Their very shape symbolizes reaching up high. Their stature symbolizes majesty, loftiness and reaching beyond the ordinary into the extraordinary. They remind us that there is an expanded perspective, a higher way to look at life.

They are also learning and teaching about coordination; for example, how to hold their body in perfect balance while they are galloping.

When a giraffe baby is born it drops an astonishing 2.5 metres to land with a thud on the ground, and then it has to struggle up by itself before it can reach for nourishment. They really do have to hold on to the vision of their divine blueprint and force themselves to stand and walk.

These animals are fascinating to watch. One of my daughters and her family once took me to the famous Longleat safari park in the UK, where there are many glorious animals freely wandering. As it was my birthday they treated me to a lettuce leaf to feed the giraffe! This lettuce leaf cost the unimaginable sum of £2. Instead of getting our cameras out our family and other tourists were laughing and gasping about the ridiculous price of a lettuce leaf. While we were distracted the nearest giraffe reached over, stuck out its black serpentine tongue and snaffled my leaf! And I didn't even have a photograph to show for it. Eventually my daughter treated me to a second lettuce leaf and we got a photo of the amazing, stately creature eating it.

VISUALIZATION TO EXPERIENCE LIFE AS A GIRAFFE

1. Find a place where you can be quiet and undisturbed.

2. Breathe comfortably and relax.

3. Ask the angel of animals, Archangel Fhelyai, to surround you in his sunshine-yellow light.

4. Then ask Archangel Jophiel, the archangel of wisdom, to touch your crown chakra. Sense it glowing and pulsing.

5. Find yourself growing taller and taller. Your neck is getting longer. So are your legs… And now you have four of them.

6. Sense yourself in the body of a giraffe.

7. A ray of pale yellow light is pouring down into your crown. It feels warm and comfortable and you sense it is full of keys and codes of information from Orion. It shows you how to use knowledge with wisdom.

8. Look down at your life. How can you use this wisdom in your home, with your family, at work and in all areas of your incarnation?

9. Think of grace and graciousness. How can you bring this quality into your daily life?

10. Simple service to nature. What can you do to help?

11. Look up and see the entire connected universe. Bring this knowledge of oneness down into your physical body.

12. Take your time to feel the wisdom of the interconnectedness of all things.

13. And now it is time to shrink down to your regular size.

14. Thank the giraffes and the Archangels Fhelyai and Jophiel.

15. Feel your fingers and toes and return to your human body.

You might like to write down what you have learned and felt.

Chapter 13

~

Goats

Message from the Goats

When you look at the world from an enlightened
perspective you see only love and peace. Our message
to you is to see through our eyes and send the
energy of oneness to everyone. You will be a bearer
of divine wisdom who can change the world.

Goats are highly intelligent animals who originate from Orion, the constellation of enlightenment and wisdom. They bring high-frequency light and wisdom into the world as well as healing, generosity and humility.

The service work of the goats is waste disposal, and they eat, digest and transmute much unwanted physical matter. At the same time, they purify the energy around the waste. They also help with local ecology. For example, there are toxic plants that other animals cannot eat that the goats will readily consume. They clear the land so that new seeds can be sown.

When their oversoul was in consultation with the Intergalactic Council and the Masters of Orion about their role on Earth, goats wanted to offer their milk and hair to humans.

It is not by chance that the female is called a nanny goat, for a nanny looks after and nurtures babies. And a nanny goat does just that.

They were also happy for their skins to be used after their death as long as this was not taken for granted.

They desired to roam free, experience the planet and act from their innate wisdom. They carry wisdom in their souls and want to spread it but most of all they seek freedom and space to be themselves.

Goats have many similarities with sheep. However, sheep come from the Pleiades as healers and are energetically very different from the goats of Orion, who spread wisdom first and act as healers as a secondary role. Sheep like to congregate in flocks. Goats too are herded into flocks, but they also like to be independent.

These special animals have a wonderful sense of balance. They love to clamber in the mountains and stand on rocks and peaks, gazing at the world and seeing all from a higher perspective. When you see a goat standing on a pinnacle it may be linking into Orion for inspiration and higher connection.

Mythology

According to Norse mythology, Thor, the god of thunder, has a chariot that is pulled by the goats Tanngrisnir and Tanngnjóstr. At night he eats the meat of the goats but leaves their bones intact, so they come back to life in the morning and pull his chariot again. One night a guest is invited to share the meal of goat. He breaks one of the goats' legs to eat the marrow. In the morning the leg is still broken and the guest has to become Thor's servant to compensate for the loss.

I interpret this as the mighty Thor can partake of the wisdom of the goats but he cannot interfere with their essence.

Pan, the God of Nature, is a ninth-dimensional Master with huge responsibilities. Because he radiates such a high frequency as he oversees the world of nature, humans have always misunderstood his role and his essence.

All of nature creates and procreates and the billy goat is very powerful with a strong creative urge. In Greek times of less spiritual understanding the god Pan was said to have the upper body of a man and the horns and lower body of a goat.

In fact, because goats carry the wisdom of Orion, they connect with Pan, the God of Nature and work with him.

Goats are working particularly energetically to lighten our planetary vibration.

When you look into a goat's eyes you see awareness, intelligence, knowing and enlightenment. However, when treated appropriately they can be loving, affectionate and loyal. With wisdom there is always love.

VISUALIZATION TO UNDERSTAND THE GOATS

1. Find a place where you can be quiet and undisturbed.

2. Relax and breathe comfortably.

3. Then tune in to the goat kingdom and see a magnificent goat standing on an outcrop of rock looking out over a valley.

4. Look through the goat's eyes at the world spread out below you.

5. Sense a golden-pink light forming in your heart. It is made up of wisdom and love and starts to radiate from your heart to the whole world.

6. You know what is happening everywhere.

7. You link into Orion, planet of wisdom and enlightenment, and a golden ray enfolds you.

8. As you see with higher eyes, you see the oneness. You have the wisdom to resolve everything with love. There is only peace. All is well.

9. In words or colours you send this message to people who are ready to hear.

10. Thank the goat and withdraw.

11. Open your eyes and send love to the goat kingdom.

Chapter 14

Guinea Pigs

Message from the Guinea Pigs

There is only love. It does not matter how big or small
you are, nor how important or insignificant you are.
When love flows from your heart it ignites the hearts
of all around you. Connect with a guinea pig and
you can do your part to illuminate the universe.

These tiny timid squeaking animals are from Venus! They are the only animal to incarnate from the planet of love and they have a huge heart-opening and healing mission on Earth. Their soul mission is to give and receive love.

Venus is the cosmic heart, the planet of love. It radiates a beautiful pink light. All the beings who originate from here carry love in their souls. This applies to humans too. I know a family where the mother, all her children and grandchildren come from Venus. They have attracted partners from Venus and they radiate open-hearted love and generosity as a family.

When the Intergalactic Council decided to send an animal to help humanity with the healing of the collective heart they realized that it would have to be one that was small and vulnerable and timid in order to engage the empathy of people. When you hold a guinea pig you receive a download of love from Venus. This special cosmic love is wonderful for healing the hearts of abused children and adults. It is no wonder that children love them. Guinea pigs have a huge part to play in the healing of our planet.

Archangel Chamuel, the pink angel of love, is in charge of South America, which is the continent of the heart. This continent is connected to Venus, so the guinea pig originally settled there where it felt at home, for there is love in the land itself. South America radiates a pink light. It is the continent that will flow most easily into the new Golden Age.

Guinea pigs do not just link people into Venus. Their light connects them through Venus to all the stars, planets and galaxies in this universe. Imagine all the filaments that connect the entire cosmos together being illuminated with pink love. That is what the guinea pigs are activating. These tiny creatures are helping to bring this vast and beautiful universe together with love, and you can do it with them.

When you are fifth-dimensional and your 12 chakras are awake and active you can connect them to certain of the stars, planets and galaxies. The guinea pigs can strengthen your connection with their radiant pink love, then help you to send out filaments of light and love to the rest of the universe.

Guinea pigs are unique, highly evolved beings of the universe. The wombats from Australia and capybaras and agouti from South America are related to them but do not hold the same qualities or soul mission.

VISUALIZATION TO CONNECT WITH LOVE
THROUGH THE GUINEA PIGS

1. Find a place where you can be quiet and undisturbed.

2. Light a candle if you can and dedicate it to lighting up the universe with love.

3. Close your eyes and breathe comfortably in and out of your heart.

4. Imagine you are holding a guinea pig and stroking it.

5. A pink light is flowing from the guinea pig and opening your heart. See or sense this happening.

6. A pure white unicorn appears in front of you and softly touches your third eye with his horn of light.

7. Instantly you sense, see or know that light from your chakras is merging with the guinea pig's pink heart energy:

   ~ Pink light is flowing from your Earth Star to Neptune and its ascended aspect Toutillay.

   ~ Pink light is flowing from your Base chakra to Saturn and its ascended aspect Quishy.

   ~ Pink light is flowing from your Sacral chakra to Sirius and its ascended aspect Lakumay.

   ~ Pink light is flowing from your Navel chakra to the Sun.

   ~ Pink light is flowing from your Solar plexus chakra to Earth and its ascended aspect Pilchay.

   ~ Pink light is flowing from your Heart chakra to Venus.

   ~ Pink light is flowing from your Throat chakra to Mercury and its ascended aspect Telephony.

   ~ Pink light is flowing from your Third eye chakra to Jupiter and its ascended aspect Jumbay.

   ~ Pink light is flowing from your Crown chakra to Uranus and its ascended aspect Curonay.

~ Pink light is flowing from your Causal chakra to the Moon.

~ Pink light is flowing from your Soul Star chakra to Orion.

~ Pink light is flowing from your Stellar Gateway chakra to Mars and its ascended aspect Nigellay.

8. Then there is an explosive burst of pink energy and connections are being made from these stars, planets and galaxies to all others in this universe.

9. You and the guinea pig are in the centre of a spirogram of pink love links.

10. Relax and be content that you have made magical connections happen. You do not realize what good you have done.

11. Thank your friend the guinea pig.

12. Return to waking consciousness. Your guinea pig has returned to the ethers but you can do this service work of love whenever you wish to.

Chapter 15

~

Hedgehogs

Message from the Hedgehogs

*Laughter heals your heart, cleanses your past
and lights up your future. Laugh at your troubles
and spread joy wherever you go. You will be
a magnet for light, love and happiness.*

These delightful little creatures originate from Orion, the constellation of wisdom and enlightenment, and touch every person and animal they meet with the frequencies of wisdom and higher awareness. They enable people to see things from a happier, higher perspective.

Despite the prickles they had to develop because of their helplessness one of the fifth-dimensional qualities they radiate is harmlessness. People sense this soul quality of harmlessness within them and also their vulnerability and love them for it.

When a creature radiates harmlessness, those around them feel safe and therefore relaxed. By their very presence hedgehogs create a relaxation response in people. They reduce stress. When people relax they become open to the information, knowledge and wisdom contained within light and are able to absorb it more easily. Hedgehogs are light initiators;

in other words they enable people to open up to accept light, which contains spiritual information and knowledge.

Their soul mission is to spread light, joy and happiness. They make people smile or laugh. This is why they often appear in children's books or on greetings cards.

Hedgehogs are very connected to Archangel Gabriel and their soul mission is to spread the light and joy of this mighty archangel wherever they go. They radiate his pure white light to everyone they meet and within that white light are held the keys and codes of happiness, joy and other ascension qualities like clarity, calm, peace and empathy.

In addition, part of the sacred seventh-dimensional geometric blueprint of Orion is encoded in their energy fields and this enables the Angels of Orion to sing over them. These angel sonics help to purify and clear the area around them.

Hedgehogs leave a trail of pure light wherever they go. Much of the world they previously inhabited is now covered in concrete so that they cannot spread their light trails over such a large area. Nevertheless, their perambulations are guided by Archangel Gabriel so they are never in a place by chance.

Their service mission is to eat unwanted grubs, and when humans started to plant hedges, hedgehogs would shelter under them and eat the slugs and snails and other insects who were there. As they walked they made little grunting sounds like tiny pigs and this is how they became known as hedge-hogs. Now they wander from place to place, often from garden to garden doing this work.

It is only now that they are becoming so rare that people recognize they are blessed indeed if a hedgehog shuffles into their garden. If you have a few moments do this meditation to help the hedgehogs, connect to Archangel Gabriel and bring more light and joy into your life and spread it to others.

VISUALIZATION TO CONNECT TO THE LIGHT AND JOY OF ARCHANGEL GABRIEL THROUGH THE HEDGEHOGS

1. Sit quietly with your eyes closed.

2. Ask Archangel Gabriel to place his huge perfect shimmering diamond over your energy fields for clarity and protection.

3. Visualize yourself sitting in a beautiful wild garden where it is quiet and peaceful.

4. Take a few moments to let the peace and stillness seep deeply into you.

5. Then be aware of a small hedgehog shuffling towards you. You may hear the rustle of the grass as he moves or hear his little grunts.

6. As he gets nearer you find yourself smiling. You may even want to laugh.

7. The angel sonics are touching you.

8. Through his presence you are receiving a download of pure white light and joy from Archangel Gabriel. It is streaming through the diamond and shimmering into your cells.

9. The Angels of Orion are surrounding you in blazing blue light. They are raising the knowledge you hold within your soul to wisdom.

10. And the hedgehog laughs, then wanders away.

11. Ask the Angels of Orion and Archangel Gabriel to look after the hedgehogs.

12. Thank them all for coming to you.

Chapter 16

~

Horses, Zebras and Donkeys

Message from the Horse Kingdom

Our hearts are huge and radiant so we spread love to all around us. In this way we heal people, other animals and the Earth. You can do this too. Just open your heart and let it blaze forth love.

Highly refined, beautiful horses incarnated from Lakumay, the ascended aspect of Sirius, during the golden era of Atlantis to serve and support humans. At this time the volunteers who seeded the great experiment of Atlantis all vibrated at the upper level of the fifth dimension. They gratefully used the horses as a method of transport and rode them bareback, directing them telepathically. In exchange the humans cared for and sheltered the animals and ensured they were well fed. There was a very strong bond of love between the horses and their human friends. It was not until Atlantis fell that horses were ridden with saddles and bridles or bred and used for heavy work.

The soul mission of these excellent, dignified creatures is service to humanity, and in return our contract is to honour and care for them.

Horses were, and still are, healers, with huge hearts. Many still demonstrate qualities of dignity, honour, love, empathy, freedom and joy. They also radiate divine feminine energy and are attuned to Angel Mary who connects with them through Venus, the cosmic heart.

As healers, horses have a great affinity with children, especially those in physical or emotional need. They can help to soothe and calm them. Like most four-legged animals, horses are very much in their bodies and also help children to relax and come fully into their bodies too. This can be really helpful for sensitive and high-frequency children who disconnect themselves energetically from Earth and become ungrounded because life is uncomfortable or the energies around them are too low but who really need to fully experience Earth. And Angel Mary works with children through horses.

When people started to bring in their 12 fifth-dimensional chakras Archangel Christiel stepped into this universe through his cross-shaped stargate on Lyra. He began to pour divine feminine light through the moon into the causal chakras of those who were ready. The causal centre is a moon-white transcendent chakra above the crown. It is through this centre that people can connect fully with angels, unicorns, illumined masters and the seventh-dimensional spirit world.

When people have raised their frequency to the higher levels of the fifth dimension, their causal chakra becomes a portal through which unicorns can step into the wavelength of Earth.

In 2012 many more people opened their causal chakras. Then, in 2015, as a result of the influence of the super moons and the ascension of Lady Gaia, a flood of Archangel Christiel's glorious divine feminine energy streamed onto people and animals alike. It particularly affected the horses who already carry divine feminine energy. It re-activated their higher mission of bringing the planet into divine masculine-feminine balance.

In the golden era of Atlantis, when it was time for a beloved horse to pass over, their human friends would watch as they translated into unicorns and ascended. I am delighted to say that a few people recently have shared with me their glorious experiences of watching their horse's spirit rising from its body, transforming into a pure white unicorn as it ascended into the light. What an awesome privilege to witness such a sight. The event is similar to the inner planes ceremony when a human ascends on passing. Angels and archangels wait to greet them. Trumpets sound across the universe and there is jubilation and delight throughout the heavens.

One of Archangel Gabriel's many tasks is to help beings in the universes to express freedom and joy, so it is not surprising that they oversee horses and help them to fulfil their potential. One of the most energy-inspiring sights is of a happy horse galloping on the sands with its mane blowing freely in the breeze.

Wild horses

Wild horses are descendants of those who were once domesticated and have escaped. They live in groups, with one male, who protects his harem of females. Young colts leave the family when they are two years old and roam with other males until they set up their own family. These horses are learning about family life and freedom. Their path does not involve humans.

Zebras

Zebras were not part of Atlantis. They came in as part of an experiment in Africa that was running concurrently with Atlantis but never became a golden age. Their intention was not to serve humanity or individuals as horses did, rather to experience life on Earth. Their service is to spread healing and balance into the land.

Zebras incarnated from Sirius and chose to be black and white, not just for camouflage, but also to express balance. As a herd and therefore part of a group consciousness, the whole mass wished to learn and teach about masculine-feminine balance. This includes the balance between freedom and conforming to the needs of the herd. They are learning that a cluster is safer than a single entity and a foal is better protected with several adults.

Archangel Gabriel works with them to help them experience joy, safety and togetherness, while Archangel Sandalphon accepts their healing energy into the Earth and spreads it through the ley lines.

Donkeys

Wild asses originally incarnated in Mesopotamia to experience life in the wilder, desert regions of Earth. They loved the mountains and sandy wildernesses.

At a soul level they wished to experience freedom, endurance, patience, lessons of living with other family members and love. They need company, and because of their big open hearts, they form strong emotional bonds. The wondrous, luminous Universal Angel Mary, who spreads love throughout the universes works with them and helps them to keep their hearts open.

Because they are sturdier and hardier than horses, over the aeons many were captured and domesticated. They were put to work by humans and like many animals are undergoing severe initiations into higher frequencies. Later they became known as donkeys.

Horses and donkeys can breed but, while horses have 64 chromosomes, donkeys have only 62. This means that cross-breeds have only 63 chromosomes, which renders them infertile.

Archangel Gabriel is also connected to donkeys and helps them to endure their crucifixions and initiations by encouraging them and trying to lift their spirits when they need it most. As we link energetically to the donkeys Archangel Gabriel automatically helps us with our own trials.

An initiation is a very demanding test. When you pass it you automatically move into a higher frequency. A crucifixion is the fourth initiation which is the test of the heart and the hardest to bear.

The Brotherhood of the Golden Robe undertake to mitigate planetary karma by passing the burdens of the world through their own energy systems. Donkeys are the animal representatives of the Brotherhood of the Golden Robe and it encourages them when you send a mental thank-you to them. Each time you do so a little golden spark flies from you and touches their heart.

It was a huge boost to the donkey world when one of their number was chosen to carry the Virgin Mary to Bethlehem. A donkey was elected to do this partly because it was the only suitable creature available but also because the spiritual hierarchy wished to acknowledge their qualities of patience, endurance and love. Whether you are a human or animal there is always a reward eventually for good actions.

Mules and hinnies

A mule is the product of a horse mare bred to a jack or male donkey. A hinny is the offspring of a stallion crossed with a female donkey.

Archangel Gabriel works with all these animals and loves and honours them all equally. Why would the soul of a horse or a donkey wish to incarnate as a mixed-breed creature?

Just as for humans, in the animal world different experiences offer a variety of choices for spiritual growth. There are always some brave souls willing to aspire to such an undertaking. And some of these animals incarnate with loving hearts in order to demonstrate compassion or the power of determination or to teach a number of other lessons.

VISUALIZATION TO UNDERSTAND HORSES

1. Find a place where you can be quiet and relaxed.

2. Draw Archangel Gabriel's diamond of purity and protection over you and breathe comfortably.

3. Imagine yourself sitting by a long sandy beach on a warm spring day. The waves are rolling into shore and you feel very comfortable.

4. A gracious horse trots along the beach towards you. It is radiating calm, love and peace.

5. It pauses beside you and telepathically invites you to ride it. Your guardian angel is close to you so you know you will be safe. You stroke your horse's nose.

6. Your angel lifts you onto the horse and sits behind you, holding you. Take a moment to bond with your steed.

7. Then you are galloping along the beach on your horse, your hair blowing in the breeze. The shallow sea is splashing under the horse's hooves.

8. Held in a pure white cocoon of love and trust you experience the exhilaration, the joy and freedom, the delight and wonder of being one with this animal. Enjoy this for as long as you like.

9. While you are riding you are receiving a download of divine feminine energy.

10. When the horse stops, pat it and thank it.

11. Let your guardian angel lift you down.

12. And now serve the horse by brushing it down, combing its mane and tail, walking it gently to a special pasture and giving it a carrot. Talk to it gently as you do so, reminding it what a magnificent animal it is.

13. Then open your eyes feeling invigorated and full of love.

Prayer of Gratitude to the Donkeys

Beloved Source I thank you for creating donkeys to show me qualities of patience, endurance and devotion to duty.

Angel Mary I thank you for pouring love into donkeys and for sending that love to me when I think of these animals.

Archangel Gabriel I thank you for supporting donkeys as they move through their initiations into ascension and for touching me with ascension light when I think of them.

Archangel Fhelyai, angel of animals, I ask you to enfold and help the donkey kingdom and touch the consciousness of humanity so that we appreciate who they truly are.

Bless the donkeys. Bless the donkeys. Bless the donkeys.

So be it.

Chapter 17

Hyenas

Message from the Hyenas

Dare to be different. However humble your position, or however ordinary your life mission, do it your way. Be true to yourself and speak your truth. People will hear you and respect you.

Hyenas are not canines and nor are they members of the cat family. These very unusual animals are more like cats though they look and act like dogs. There are striped hyenas, spotted ones, known as the laughing hyena, and brown ones.

They are found in Asia and Europe but mostly in Africa and they incarnated with a complex soul mission. Originating in Uranus, they step their energy down through Sirius in order to come to Earth. Beings from Uranus come to bring in change and often behave in bizarre or different ways, challenging the norms and bringing about social change. Within the animal kingdom hyenas fulfil this description.

Archangel Jophiel works with them to keep their connection to Uranus clear.

Their service mission is rather like that of rats who come to clear up all leftovers so that our planet is kept clean, physically and energetically.

The soul mission of hyenas is to balance their qualities. They have a reputation for being cowardly and timid yet at the same time they can be bold and dangerous, being known to attack humans as well as other animals.

Clarity of communication is one of their strengths. They use their tails to advertise their intentions. When it is carried straight, their intention is to attack. Excitement is shown by their tail being held up and forward over their back. If feeling comfortable their tail hangs down and fear is indicated by tucking their tail between their legs.

Hyenas are highly sociable and social, very intelligent animals. They are learning and teaching about love and about family. Cubs are raised in a den in the centre of their territory, which is also their community meeting place. The entrances are connected to a complex series of underground tunnels. They are extremely disciplined and have a very tight social structure where every animal knows their exact position. They form strong, enduring friendships with certain members of their clan, just as humans can do in a community. When people have peaceful intentions hyenas allow them to befriend them. As more and more people are raising their frequency there are more reports of human friendship with hyenas.

Originating as they do from Uranus, they do things differently. They are testing the norms on Earth. For example, quite unusually females are larger and heavier than the males. Their clans of about 80 hyenas are led by females. Their cubs are born with their eyes open. They are both scavengers and skilful hunters and they will eat almost anything as they learn about expanding their digestive abilities. They even have long front legs and short back ones, which is an experiment to see how agile they can be with this variant. In fact, they can walk, trot or run with ease.

They are developing their throat chakras with a variety of sounds and calls, including wailing, howling, screaming and laughter. There are many videos on the Internet of the extraordinary animal lover Kevin Richardson interacting with hyenas. He vigorously strokes their throats and says this is their favourite place to be tickled. This suggests that these animals are expanding their throat centres, the chakra of honesty, truth, higher connections, courage and communication.

Hyenas are third-dimensional. When they ascend into the fifth dimension, they will be able to tune in to the ascended aspect of Uranus, which is Curonay. Then they will access light from there that contains higher spiritual knowledge and information. This will bring about change on Earth in line with the fifth-dimensional ascended blueprint. Hyenas are harbingers of change.

VISUALIZATION TO CONNECT TO URANUS AND ITS ASCENDED ASPECT, CURONAY, THROUGH HYENAS

1. Find a place where you can be quiet and undisturbed.

2. If possible light a candle to raise the frequency.

3. Set your intention to connect to Archangel Jophiel through the hyenas and then to link into Uranus and its ascended aspect Curonay.

4. Find yourself sitting in an unexpected place, where everything is very beautiful but different.

5. You may be surprised to find a glorious luminous crystal-yellow Archangel beside you, with its hands on the crown of your head. This is Archangel Jophiel. Sense the warmth, the peace and the safety.

6. And a spotted hyena is loping towards you, greeting you in a very benign and friendly way.

7. Stroke his throat and sense him relax even more until he lies beside you.

8. And now a shimmering, shining crystal-yellow ray of light beams from Archangel Jophiel surrounding the hyena and you. Then it reaches out through the universe to Uranus and then to Curonay.

9. Suddenly you see your whole life transforming. Things you have taken for granted are changing. You see new and unexpected things happening for you. Take your time to explore these.

10. And now you become aware of exciting changes in the world around you as preparations for the new Golden Age accelerate. Take some time to explore the possibilities.

11. Through your connection to the hyena and Archangel Jophiel, to Uranus and Curonay, the keys and codes of new and unexpected beneficial changes have been triggered.

12. Thank them all. Then open your eyes.

13. Expect transformation.

Chapter 18

Kangaroos and Wallabies

Message from the Kangaroos and Wallabies

We want to remind you that when you are vulnerable you become sensitive to the needs of others and the earth itself. This enhances your divine feminine light. And when you balance this with your masculine energy you become a great force for good.

Lemuria was the Golden Age after Mu and before Atlantis. The amazing and unique kangaroos and wallabies originally came to Earth at the end of the Golden Age of Lemuria. The Lemurians were etheric beings and never took physical bodies. However, they passionately loved the planet and nature. Even then they knew that there would be a 20-year period between 2012, the final end of the Age of Atlantis, and 2032 when the next golden age begins. So they left an incredible legacy of special Lemurian crystals specifically created to help humans through this current challenging 20-year period. They left an etheric library full of information about nature, the planet and our relationship with other planetary systems and especially the four ascension stars, planets and constellations, Neptune, Orion, the Pleiades and Sirius. When people are ready they can access this information.

The Aborigines and the kangaroos and wallabies incarnated at the same time in order to ground the wisdom and energy of Lemuria. They were able to tune from a distance in to the Lemurian crystals to access the information they needed for survival and to honour the planet.

The Aborigines are attuned to the Sun and through it to the Great Central Sun, the source of light for this universe. This is a masculine energy which balances their feminine orientation.

The kangaroos and wallabies originate from Nigellay, the ascended aspect of Mars, and they carry the qualities of the peaceful warrior.

Neither the Aborigines nor the kangaroos were part of the Atlantean experiment but were participating in another vision set in Australia. Because the ecosystem and structure of the soil is very fragile in Australia, Source designed the kangaroos to use their kundalini, which is the life force held in the base of the spine, in a different way from other animals, so that they would be light on the land. These animals demonstrate that kundalini can be used to bound so that the soil structure is not damaged.

Kangaroos are healers. Because of their love of nature and Earth itself they heal the land wherever they go. They send Lemurian healing down the ley lines, keeping them light and clear. They are attuned to the Angels of Lemuria and bring their pure white-gold healing light down through their chakra systems into Earth. Wherever possible they are enabling the ley lines to carry a fifth-dimensional frequency.

The Lemurians drew the light and love of Source down through the cosmic heart into Earth itself. The kangaroos too are able to link into the cosmic heart and bring the light and love down through their hearts into the Earth. Mother Mary oversaw the Lemurian influence on Earth and the kangaroos are attuned to this great master, who works with the light of the cosmic Christ. It is her tender, pure love that surrounds the mother kangaroo and her very vulnerable joey in aquamarine light to enable them to bond and survive.

Because kangaroos and wallabies originate from the ascended aspect of Mars, the planet that spreads the qualities of the peaceful warrior throughout the world, they hold qualities of strength, courage, determination, leadership, the power to protect those weaker than themselves and balanced masculine energy within their auric fields. In equal balance they hold the divine feminine qualities of tenderness, love, wisdom, ability to nurture and care for the vulnerable. This perfect balance of masculine and feminine energy makes them stand out in the animal kingdom.

The males demonstrate their masculine power by the way they fiercely protect themselves and their young and fight for mating rights. As part of this particular experiment it was decided to see how the maternal instinct of a doe would manage with an incredibly vulnerable joey. The baby is about the size of a bean or a peanut, hairless and completely helpless, except for its instinct to climb into the mother's pouch, where it remains for nine months. And the mothers have well-developed maternal instincts. They are gentle and nurturing of their vulnerable young. When the young one is mature enough the mother encourages it to venture out for short periods, while carefully protecting it.

The Aborigines and the kangaroos and wallabies had a special symbiotic relationship. They were able to communicate telepathically. They honoured, respected and loved each other. If the Aborigines needed meat for survival a weak kangaroo who was ready to go home would signal this telepathically to the hunters and offer himself to them. This sacrifice would be recorded and duly rewarded on the animal's spiritual journey.

Kangaroos are extremely sensitive. They pick up the vibrations of everything around them – from the growth of plants, to the energy of the wind and the movements within the earth itself. When everything is in harmony it keeps them totally in balance. They are particularly sensitive to the vibrations of humans and if people are negative this can knock them off centre.

The archangel who overlights Australia is Archangel Roquiel, whose etheric retreat is over Uluru. She works with the divine feminine vibration of black. And deep within the planet she coordinates with Archangel Sandalphon to keep the energy round the Earth Star chakras of humanity clear. Even if people are spiritually asleep she is working to prepare the energy around their Earth Stars so that when they are ready the light can pour from the glorious heart of Source through the person and enter the earth.

At the same time Archangel Gersisa is helping balance and heal Earth by holding the Lemurian wisdom steady in the centre, in Hollow Earth.

Together they keep the ley lines of Australia clear and high-frequency.

Kangaroos are connected to these three archangels. Every time they bounce on the earth there is a two-way energy exchange. The archangels support the animals while the kangaroos receive a boost of light from the archangels.

If a ley line is blocked the archangels will communicate to the kangaroos who will be drawn there to heal it.

These extraordinary creatures really are links between heaven and Earth and as high-frequency beings from the ascended aspect of Mars, they need to live in a calm, centred way in order to fulfil their mission of spreading peace and healing on Earth.

VISUALIZATION TO CONNECT WITH THE KANGAROOS

1. Find a place where you can be quiet and undisturbed.

2. Ask Archangel Michael to protect you and light up the divine masculine qualities in your aura.

3. Ask the Angel Mary to fill you with love and light up the divine feminine qualities in your aura.

4. Take a moment to imagine you are touching the Earth. How does it feel? What does it need?

5. Nurture it. Give it what it needs.

6. How does the Earth need to be protected? Use your masculine energy to do what needs to be done.

7. Take a moment to think of your friends and family. How do they feel? What do they need?

8. Nurture them. Give them what they need.

9. And now how do your friends and family need to be protected? Use your masculine energy to do what needs to be done.

10. Picture a kangaroo in front of you and thank it for its influence.

11. Let its energy light up and balance your energies.

12. Open your eyes and remember the kangaroos when you need to balance.

Chapter 19

Llamas and Alpacas

Message from the Llamas and Alpacas

*When your heart is open and your intention pure, you can make
miracles happen. Think of us and we will automatically raise
your frequency. We will connect you to the cosmic heart and
enfold you in the golden Christ Light. Then expect miracles.*

Llamas are relatives of camels though they do not have a hump
and spiritually they are quite different. They originate from
Sirius. They incarnated into South America, which is governed by
Venus, the planet of love, so they also have a strong connection
with that planet. They carry the 33-petalled pink-and-white rose
in their auras and radiate Christ Light. This helps to keep open
the hearts of the people with whom they live.

They incarnated to serve the people who lived in the
Andes and have always done so with grace. They offer their
beautiful and luxurious wool to them. In addition, llamas have
enormous strength and willingly allow themselves to be used
as pack animals to help the humans they live with. However,
if overloaded, they will refuse to carry the burden and may
spit, hiss or kick at their owners until it is removed. They are
learning and teaching about the setting of boundaries.

Unlike camels, llamas cannot store water, so they must drink frequently and need to be close to water.

These gentle animals are particularly intelligent, open-hearted and loving. As long as they are treated fairly they respond by giving. They are happy to give their wool. They are even content to give their hides to make leather after they die but would like to be asked. Sometimes they are eaten by their owners and this is definitely not part of their contract.

Llamas are very sociable and enjoy being in the company of other llamas. This gives them encouragement and helps them keep their frequency fifth-dimensional.

They are quiet, gentle and understanding, especially with those in need. They are very patient with ill, weak or mentally incapacitated people and their high frequency enables them to raise the energies of such people and offer them healing. All llamas are heart healers.

They bond closely with any animals they are charged with looking after and because they are dedicated, loyal and obedient they make excellent guard animals.

Llamas have always been domesticated and in service. Their wild ancestors, the vicuna, incarnate from Sirius and are third-dimensional. They spread joy and light into the land but do not have the ascended qualities or love of the llamas.

Alpacas

Alpacas are smaller than the llamas but spiritually they are very similar, with warm loving hearts and a kind, patient and gentle disposition. They were domesticated by the Incas for their wool. They also make devoted pets.

Like llamas they are great heart healers and spread healing to people and into the land wherever they are.

My friend Rosemary Stephenson has two alpacas who bring her great joy. Though they are placid and friendly animals, twice thieves have broken in at night and tried to take them and each time the larger one has fought them off. They are fiercely protective of their homes and their companions.

VISUALIZATION TO CONNECT WITH LLAMAS (OR ALPACAS)

1. Find a place where you can be quiet and undisturbed.

2. Invoke the Gold Ray of Christ and feel its golden light flowing over and through you.

3. Imagine you are sitting on a mountainside in the Andes. The sky is blue and the air pure and clear.

4. A llama or an alpaca is quietly, lovingly approaching you.

5. It stands beside you, looking at you with its huge, dark, soft eyes. You reach up and gently stroke its wool.

6. You sense a beautiful pink light radiating from its heart. This light flows round you and cocoons you in a blanket of pink peace.

7. Relax in the cocoon for you are receiving heart healing that spreads through your body.

8. Thank the llama or alpaca for coming to you and know you are connected.

9. Open your eyes and let the soft healing stay with you.

Chapter 20

~

Monkeys and Apes

Message from the Monkeys and Apes

We are here to be – to be one with nature and the trees.
To live in open-hearted integrity with all creatures. We do
not try to think or rationalize, merely to experience what life
has to offer. Our message to you is to open your heart and
your right brain and you too will experience oneness.

All monkeys and apes, including lemurs, bush babies, gorillas and chimpanzees, are highly evolved beings. They originate from the tenth-dimensional universe of Shekinah, where the energy is pure love and light, more beautiful and glorious than anything we can imagine. They step their energy down through the healing star cluster of the Pleiades.

While any being from the tenth dimension carries healing in their fields, because monkeys and apes descend through the Pleiades, healing is one of their dominant gifts. They express this through their energy fields but also through their chatter. This is much more than verbal communication; through it they share information from the angels and other elementals and spread it to the trees, animals, birds and even humans.

These diverse animals incarnate in order to experience and learn about those elements that are not available in their home universe, such as fun, family life, connection to trees, food and the senses. However, they are learning with the right brain and the heart, not the left brain and the head. This means that though they may be spiritually much more evolved than many humans, they have not focused on or developed the same intellectual capacity. They follow their hearts not their heads, and their instincts rather than logical outcomes. They are intentionally learning about life on Earth with the heart-centred qualities of unconditional love and acceptance, loyalty, trust, wisdom, caring, peace, togetherness and companionship. They are demonstrating to us many of the divine feminine qualities that we need to incorporate in the new Golden Age.

They are so highly evolved that they would not allow themselves to be caught or killed unless it was for a higher purpose. They are hoping to trigger compassion or even pity for they usually make this sacrifice in order to touch and open people's hearts. While this is not part of their soul mission it has become part of their service work.

Monkeys show us that it is possible to use kundalini, or vital life force, to swing through the trees. They are very relaxed and happy up in the trees for air is their element. Only gorillas are relaxed and comfortable on the ground. Other monkeys show us that it is not necessary to be physically on the ground to be part of this planet. Whether they touch Mother Earth or not, they still receive a loving invitation from Lady Gaia to incarnate for an experience here. Monkeys are vulnerable and uncomfortable when out of their own particular element, though they may wish at a soul level to experience fire, water and earth. These are not available in the universe of Shekinah.

All monkeys are incredibly curious about anything on Earth. Because I was brought up in India where there are many monkeys my mother would often regale us with her monkey stories. Apparently my mother used to keep Epsom salts in their bathroom cabinet. One day a group of monkeys crept into the house and, being inquisitive, they opened the bathroom cabinet. They took the Epsom salts and ate the contents of the packet. Next morning the monkeys were seen lying on the lawn groaning and rubbing their stomachs (or so the story goes). This was drummed into us as a lesson not to take anything from the medicine chest.

All monkeys and apes are totally in tune with the wisdom of the trees, for trees are ancient, wise sentient beings with a seventh-dimensional blueprint.

They hold the knowledge of their local areas. When a being sings with an open heart the angels can create sonics over them. And the diverse sounds made by monkeys and apes who have open hearts enable the angels to send sonics that help the trees to grow and flourish. In response, the trees send energy back to them as they do to humans. Trees cleanse the energy in the areas where they grow and monkeys and apes help them with this. While humans aim and aspire to understand oneness, the monkeys and apes truly experience it.

Most of the creatures who enter Earth via the Pleiades come through a high-frequency portal at Mount Shasta, California, which is overseen by Archangel Gabriel. Monkeys and apes are no exception. Because of this the Angels of the Pleiades watch over them from a distance as does Archangel Gabriel. The great Archangel Metatron also works with them, for monkeys and apes demonstrate the qualities of the divine feminine that are so needed as we accelerate into the fifth dimension.

VISUALIZATION TO CONNECT WITH MONKEYS AND APES

1. Find a place where you can be quiet and undisturbed.

2. If possible light a candle and dedicate it to oneness.

3. Imagine yourself sitting under a beautiful tropical tree with sunlight filtering through its branches. You feel totally safe.

4. You hear the chattering of monkeys and a cheeky face peers at you through the leaves.

5. Then you see many monkeys swinging and leaping joyfully from branch to branch.

6. One of them swings down and sits quietly in front of you. You notice its heart centre is wide open and radiating.

7. You become aware of golden filaments of light reaching from its heart and touching you, so that you feel the love coming to you.

8. The filaments are reaching out and touching the trees, the flowers, other monkeys and all the birds and animals. Love is flowing through the links.

9. You are in the centre of a web of light and love.

10. You are part of the oneness. Rest in this feeling and keep it in your heart.

11. Thank the monkey and open your eyes.

12. Know that you can recreate the feeling of oneness wherever you are.

Chapter 21

~

Pandas

Message from the Pandas

When you think of us you receive healing from the Pleiades.
And love from the cosmic heart touches your heart.

Pandas originate from the Pleiades star cluster. It radiates divine feminine light and unimaginable blue healing energy. All the beings, people, animals, insects or aquatic creatures, who originate from here are heart healers. A vast blue etheric rose with 33 open petals lies between Source and the Pleiades. Pure healing love pours down from Source through the rose to the Masters and Angels of the Pleiades. They, in turn, step the frequency down and pass it on to creatures and other planes of existence.

Pandas carry the symbol of the blue rose of the Pleiades in their aura. This means that pure Source healing is stepped down through the 33-petalled rose into their energy fields and they spread it to everyone and everything in their vicinity. You can also tune in to this healing light by seeing, thinking of or looking at a picture of a panda.

It is not by chance that pandas are black and white. This colouring was deliberately chosen by the oversoul of the pandas to demonstrate that their masculine and feminine energy is perfectly in balance and that not everything is one extreme or another. They encourage others to look with enlightened eyes. In doing so they help everyone bring things into balance.

While they are generally passive, if they are provoked they are highly dangerous. They demonstrate their masculine power by being formidable creatures who can attack with their paws, large teeth and great strength. They can deliver one of the most powerful bites of any animal. This has been developed to allow them to crack their way into the extremely tough sheath of bamboo.

Their feminine side is shown by their incredible maternal instinct. The way they care for their vulnerable offspring is exemplary. At birth the cub is totally helpless. A newborn cub weighs only a few grams and is ridiculously tiny, pink, hairless and blind. Along with the kangaroo or opossum the panda is the smallest mammal when newborn relative to the size of its mother. The mother has to tend it with enormous care to ensure its survival. Before they came to Earth the vulnerability of the newborn panda was decided by the Masters of the Pleiades in conjunction with the Intergalactic Council. This choice was made specifically to test the feminine qualities of the female panda for caring, tenacity, love, maternal instinct, patience and healing.

The endangered giant pandas are solitary animals who now live in a few mountain ranges in central China. They demonstrate that it is absolutely fine to walk alone on your spiritual path. Farming, deforestation and other development has driven the giant panda out of the lowlands where it used to live. If only humans understood the incredible healing mission these beautiful animals have undertaken, we would ensure they had the space they need.

Archangel Jophiel, the angel of wisdom, is the archangel in overall charge of China. He also watches over the pandas and brings his wisdom down through them.

Pandas are also attuned to Archangel Sandalphon, who takes this wisdom and passes it through the planetary Earth Star chakra to Lady Gaia.

The mighty Universal Angel Mary works with pandas. She helps to connect them to Venus, the cosmic heart, and through the pandas she helps to link people everywhere to the cosmic heart.

Their soul mission is to bring heart healing to people, animals and places on our planet. They hold such healing light in their auras that it actively touches and lights up those around them. Anyone in the presence of a panda or who thinks of one draws this healing energy from them. They maintain this by being at peace and holding truth, innocence and purity in their hearts.

VISUALIZATION TO CONNECT WITH THE PANDAS

1. Find a place where you can be relaxed and undisturbed.
2. Breathe comfortably and allow yourself to let go.
3. You find yourself in the soft clear green light of a beautiful mountain in China. You are safe and happy.
4. Your guardian angel is gently placing a young panda into your arms.
5. It is soft and warm. Just stroke and cuddle the baby panda and feel your heart opening.
6. The great Universal Angel Mary is pouring a ray of shimmering pink light over you, holding you and the panda in a shaft of glorious pink energy. The shaft goes to the cosmic heart.
7. Find yourself travelling with the panda gently up the shaft into a vast pink rose, the cosmic heart.

8. The 33 soft velvety petals open as you rest in the centre of them, quietly holding the panda.

9. The Angel Mary touches your heart and opens it wider.

10. Beautiful blue Angels of the Pleiades sing over you as you lie cradled in the rose.

11. At last your guardian angel conducts you back down the shaft to where you started.

12. Every time you think of a panda your heart opens and is activated with love.

Chapter 22

~

Pigs

Message from the Pigs

There is nothing more important than love. When your heart is pure you automatically spread truth and healing for that is love. It is the gift we offer and we ask you to value it. Then you will value us.

Pigs arrived on this planet at the start of the golden era of Atlantis with a mission to serve humanity. They incarnated from the Pleiades, the star cluster of healing.

Pigs carry a blue rose in their aura and when they are born the blue rose is tiny over their heart. As they mature the blue rose, energetic symbol of love and healing, expands round their aura and they spread heart healing wherever they go. They help to keep the land pure and clear.

People tend to think of Golden Atlantis as a time of wondrous technology, of great and advanced inventions and extraordinary psychic gifts and talents and this is true. However, all of this was only developed because the hearts of the inhabitants were open and fifth-dimensional and they could be trusted to use these great abilities for the highest good.

Originally, during that fifth-dimensional era, pigs arrived as household pets. They offered love and healing to keep the frequency of the heart energy of the home as high as it could possibly be. They also served in an ecological capacity by eating the leftovers.

After their death the people used their soft skins to make shoes and other useful items. Before they took their skins they asked permission from the spirit of the pig. They would never take anything without prior approval.

In exchange for the service they offered, the pigs were given shelter, respected, honoured and cared for. People recognized it was a privilege to have such an evolved and magnificent animal as part of their family.

Pigs incarnated originally to offer their hearts and it is interesting that now, as the frequency is starting to rise again, people are once again choosing pigs as pets in their homes.

Pigs are naturally fastidious and clean animals. It has been an insult to their soul to be left to lie in muddy conditions and even worse to be given a reputation for being dirty creatures when they are no such thing. Through them love from the blue rose goes deep into the Earth and also into the ley lines to send healing into them.

In other parts of the world different experiments were taking place. Wild pigs and boars on other continents also come from the Pleiades but the blue rose in their aura carries a much lower frequency. Nevertheless, they still spread some healing and help to hold the heart energy, but not to the same degree as the domestic pigs that came into Atlantis.

Although the energy has devolved as far as it has, the pigs everywhere are trying valiantly to do their loving work. However, they never anticipated their flesh would be used to feed humans and they will not tolerate this much longer.

Like all animals from the Pleiades pigs are connected to the healing Angels of the Pleiades and also Mother Mary. They are also linked to Archangel Gabriel, who touches them with clarity and joy. Because humanity has abused these beautiful creatures so much, Archangel Fhelyai, the angel of animals, and Archangel Uriel are working closely with them to raise their confidence again. This doesn't apply only to pigs. If a human was subjected to the treatment that we give to pigs their confidence would be rock bottom. So it is with many animals, and Archangel Uriel is trying to touch as many of them as possible to help them restore their inner self-worth. If you can send a prayer to Archangel Uriel to increase the self-worth, self-value, self-esteem of animals that would be a really important and helpful offering.

Prayer to Archangel Uriel

Beloved Archangel Uriel,

I ask from the depth of my loving heart that you touch and surround all the animals in the world, especially the pigs, with your golden light. Please help to restore their confidence, self-respect, self-value and self-worth so that they can fulfil their missions with dignity.

I ask this in the name of love and peace on Earth.

So be it.

VISUALIZATION TO CONNECT WITH THE PIGS

1. Find a place where you can be quiet and undisturbed.
2. Close your eyes and breathe comfortably until you feel really relaxed.
3. Imagine you are in your home. Look round it and sense the energy.
4. There is a knock on your door and when you open it you find your guardian angel waiting.
5. It is holding an adorable small pink piglet in its arms.

6. Very gently and lovingly your guardian angel enters and places the piglet in the middle of your sitting room.

7. You notice its aura is clear blue. There is a glorious blue rose with 33 open petals floating above it.

8. A ray of blue healing light pours down through the open rose into the piglet and spreads out until it fills the room.

9. You notice everyone and everything in the room lighting up with blue healing light.

10. The blue light is gently enveloping you and you breathe the healing into your cells.

11. The blue light is moving deep into the earth beneath your home and healing the land you live on.

12. If you wish, stroke or cuddle the piglet. You may receive a message from it.

13. When it is time for it to depart, thank it for coming to you.

14. Thank the entire pig kingdom.

15. Open your eyes and see pigs in a very different light.

Chapter 23

Rabbits and Hares

Message from the Rabbits and Hares

Even if you feel you are insignificant, nevertheless
you may have a great and important soul mission.
Working with others you can make magic happen.

Rabbits originate from Orion, the constellation of wisdom and enlightenment. All beings from here carry qualities of the divine feminine, light and joy as well as wisdom in their energy fields and the rabbits clearly demonstrate this. They also radiate qualities of gentleness, softness, caring, empathy, fun and other divine feminine attributes.

In the era of Golden Atlantis every home had a cat, dogs and a rabbit. The cat watched over the energy of the home and protected it. There could be three dogs in a house for each child had one and learned to look after it. The dog protected the child and went to school with it. The rabbit also protected the child, for with their female, mothering energy they can be formidable in guarding their loved ones. However, the rabbit stayed at home, maintaining the energy there with the cat. Because cats and rabbits both come from Orion, though they have been allocated different roles on Earth, they have an affinity which at that time was openly recognized. They would often be seen telepathically conversing.

Rabbits are pure, light, cuddly and fluffy. Children would hug them when they needed comfort. At the same time, they are practical, helpful and caring. They know exactly what is happening in the energy fields of humans and other animal species alike. If someone needs support and comfort or if they feel hurt or betrayed, as they cuddle a rabbit, it can help to heal their heart. As healers of the heart they have much to offer for, coming from Orion, they heal with wisdom as well as love.

Knowledge is knowing the facts. Wisdom is having the insight, overall perspective and love to know how to handle the situation in the best possible way.

These wise little creatures are very connected to the Song of the Earth. Every sentient being emits musical notes. Mountains seamed with clear crystals sound pure clear notes. Clean oceans and rivers play beautiful harmonies. Every tree, rock and animal adds to melody of the whole. And a peaceful planet sounds like an orchestra gliding through space.

When you feel in harmony you too add to the beauty and vibrancy of the planetary orchestra.

However, at present Earth as a whole is out of tune and sounds a discordant note as it floats through the universe. As the frequency of the planet and the universe rises, everything is rapidly transforming and Earth will be at peace and in harmony soon after the new Golden Age starts in 2032.

Rabbits tune in to the real signature tune of Earth being sung by Lady Gaia. The rabbit is a small but special creature and it relays the Song of the Earth through its auric field. Part of its soul mission is to help others come into harmony with it. One drop of oil soothes troubled waters; high frequencies consume lower ones; pure clear notes raise the whole choir into harmony; and rabbits are attuned to the Song of the Earth to teach us all to ascend beautifully.

This, together with the wisdom that rabbits spread through their energy fields to others, is a huge service offering during their incarnation. They are trying to bring the people, other animals, earth, elementals, grass, flowers, trees, rivers and seas into harmonic alignment.

Because rabbits are tuned to the Song of the Earth, they can hear when a human or a predator is approaching, for their vibrations affect the music. This ability protects them, warning them of danger. At the same time the rabbits valiantly try to raise the lower frequencies around humans and predators to a higher level.

Rabbits work with Archangel Gabriel, a mighty messenger of light, to spread purity, clarity, light and joy wherever they go.

Where there is harmony, sacred geometry and intention, the angels sing over that place and change the sound into angel sonics. Rabbits carry sacred geometric wisdom in their auras so the angels sing harmonics over them. As a result, through these furry little creatures, angel sonics spread over the pastures.

Archangel Sandalphon is known as the angel of music for he understands the harmonics of creation. Through the rabbits he attunes with Archangel Gabriel to connect the sonics of the Song of the Earth with the Music of the Spheres. These are the divinely perfect harmonies created by the movements of all celestial bodies. This helps to hold in place the seventh-dimensional blueprint for Earth as a vision of our divine potential.

Unicorns are drawn to the purity and innocence of these animals. If you stroke a rabbit with love a unicorn may shower a blessing onto you. If you see a field full of bobtails scampering about there will often be a unicorn pouring light down onto them. This light is taken into their burrows and into the land itself. In this way the rabbits bring the highest light into the ground and anchor it there.

Rabbits have proliferated in their efforts to bring the land itself into the fifth dimension. They will gather in places that need their energy, where they can focus the harmonics of the Song of the Earth. Even though humans curse them and shoot them, and other animals predate on them, rabbits courageously continue with their mission. They are valiant little light workers.

VISUALIZATION TO CONNECT WITH THE RABBITS

1. Find a place where you can be quiet and undisturbed.

2. Archangel Michael places his blue cloak of protection around you.

3. Imagine yourself sitting in a beautiful emerald-green meadow, dotted with colourful, fragrant wild flowers.

4. A soft furry rabbit approaches you and looks at you with soft, loving, brown eyes.

5. Pick it up and cuddle the soft, furry animal. If you wish to you can mentally tell it your problems.

6. Take your time to stroke the rabbit while the animal radiates love, healing and wisdom to you.

7. Call in Archangel Gabriel. See his pure white light approaching and sense him lighting you up.

8. Now mentally call in Archangel Sandalphon. See his silver light approaching you, then merge with you.

9. You may become aware of the Song of the Earth. Even if you can't hear it, the vibration is flowing through you, bringing you into harmony.

10. And now the light of Archangels Gabriel and Sandalphon is connecting you to the Music of the Spheres. Feel the entire universe aligning into harmony.

11. A unicorn showers blessings onto you and the rabbit.

12. Thank the rabbit, Archangels Gabriel and Sandalphon and the unicorns.

13. Then open your eyes as you feel yourself in harmony.

Hares

Despite their similarity hares come from Sirius, while rabbits originate from Orion. Hares carry very ancient knowledge about the Earth within the sacred geometry of their blueprint. Like many animals they are here to learn and teach about love, survival and trust in a physical body. Their mission is to spread into the ground and to every creature and person they meet the knowledge that they hold about ancient Earth.

They link with Archangel Uriel, the archangel in charge of the solar plexus, who is helping them to gain confidence in themselves, so that they can stand in their power. When they can do this and radiate a golden solar plexus and humanity reaches the same level, they will bring forward ancient wisdom and spread it.

I once saw two hares in my garden, standing tall, proud and very still. They didn't dance or box as I hoped they might. Nevertheless, I felt it was a special privilege that they entered my garden and connected energetically with me. We stood silently looking at each other for some time, then they quietly disappeared.

Chapter 24

Rats, Mice and Hamsters

Message from the Rats, Mice and Hamsters

*If you feel misunderstood remember your life has a higher purpose.
Hold your vision however difficult this may seem and the universe
will bring you your due tribute and rewards when the time is right.*

Rats

A friend of mine visited a beauty spot and was shocked to see
rubbish and debris lying around everywhere. She felt pretty
annoyed at the people who had left it. As she was about to
leave a clear voice in her head said, 'And what about the psychic
rubbish you leave around with your judgemental thoughts?'

She stopped still, completely stunned, as she realized the
rightness of this.

Whenever anyone thinks an angry, fearful, judgemental
or otherwise negative thought it is left for some being to
transmute, just as the physical debris we discard has to be
cleared up and disposed of.

Rats are highly evolved and intelligent creatures with big
hearts. They originate on Neptune. Thousands of years ago the
oversoul of the rats stepped forward in response to a clarion

147

call for assistance and volunteered in good faith to incarnate on Earth to clear up and transmute the psychic and physical rubbish created by humans. To do this they would take the garbage into their bodies, then transmute and purify all negative energy. This highly spiritual service work was much appreciated by humans and the universe.

For aeons this system worked very well. The payback for the rats was the gratitude they received, which kept their hearts open, and the learnings that they could take back with them to Neptune.

Unfortunately, as humans became more unconscious about their surroundings and their beautiful planet they started to produce more and more rubbish and create more sewage until the rats were in overload. Now rats could no longer transmute the sheer volume of stuff. They decided to send to Neptune for more of their kind to help them. Human gratitude turned to dislike.

Because rats were taking in so much human negativity it started to cause disease in their bodies. Humans became afraid of catching Weil's disease. Dislike then turned to fear and hatred.

At last people decided there were too many rats and that they should be culled. And so a battle started between the rats, who were trying to fulfil their mission, and humans, who wanted to destroy them without taking responsibility for the garbage and negativity they were creating.

Now rats too live their lives in fear – and fear means that they cannot transform, purify and transmute the lower energies into love.

It is time for us to recognize the soul mission of the rats and what they are trying to do to help the planet. The first step is to take responsibility for the rubbish we leave, both physical and psychic.

Cockroaches, also from Neptune, are endeavouring to fulfil the same mission for the insect world.

The situation has become so overwhelming on Earth that Archangels Purlimiek and Butyalil together have invited esaks and kyhils, who are water elementals, into the planet from another universe. These are tiny elementals who consume and transmute all kinds of negativity. I have seen them in Orb photographs beavering away where drugs have been consumed as well as where people have a low frequency or are leaving a lot of negativity around. They are trying to support the rats.

Archangels Zadkiel and Gabriel work with the rat kingdom. Archangel Zadkiel is the Archangel of transmutation and mercy. He and his angels are violet and their light transmutes and purifies all it touches with the Violet Flame. At one time they had a wonderful symbiotic relationship with the rats and they would mutually assist each other with their service mission.

Archangel Gabriel is the pure white Archangel of purification and clarity. He works with the Cosmic Diamond to cut away all lower energies in the brilliant facets of his diamond light. Now that Archangels Gabriel and Zadkiel are working together they have formed the Cosmic Diamond Violet Flame and this extraordinary purifying and transmuting light is infinitely more powerful than the Violet Flame or Cosmic Diamond alone. It is a potent clearance tool. The Archangels are trying to use it to help the rats but often cannot reach them because their frequency has become too low.

Humans can help by asking the fire dragons or violet dragons to go to the rats, then burn up and transmute the lower energy around them. Then, at last, the Archangels can use the Cosmic Diamond Violet Flame to help them.

Pet rats who are well cared for are extremely bright. They are loved and respected by their owners and this love is helping to transmute some of the fear generated by humans and wild rats.

Visualization to Help the Rats

1. Light a candle if possible and find somewhere that you can be undisturbed.

2. Sit quietly and focus on your breathing to calm your mind.

3. Find yourself in a sunny spot by a riverbank, watching the water peacefully flowing.

4. You are totally safe here. Nothing can hurt or harm you.

5. A rat approaches and sits a metre or so away from you. He is waiting for you to speak.

6. Mentally apologize to him for all that humanity has perpetrated on rats.

7. Tell him you appreciate all that rats have done to clear and transmute the rubbish and negative energy of humans. Thank him for their service.

8. Ask him to take this message back to the rat kingdom.

9. Invoke the fire dragons and ask them to burn up the lower energy where rats live.

10. Call in Archangels Gabriel and Zadkiel and ask them to place the Cosmic Diamond Violet Flame over all the rats. Watch the energies rising.

11. Thank the rats, the dragons and Archangels Gabriel and Zadkiel.

Mice

Mice fulfil the same purpose as rats though they have a gentler energy and have not been as affected by the anger of humans as rats. Nevertheless, they are trying to clear and transmute our rubbish and leftovers. Their offer of service did not include allowing their bodies to be used for research. That was never on offer and is creating not just pain, but even agony for the animals, and also great karma for the perpetrators and often for the users of the products.

Archangels Zadkiel and Gabriel also work with mice.

Hamsters

Because hamsters breed copiously they have been frequently used by humans for laboratory experiments. By a quirk of human sensibility, they are also beloved pets.

They came to Earth to teach and learn about what we would call civilized living. Their underground burrows have a front and back door, bedroom, store room and separate toilet. They carry food in their cheek pouches to their homes for they need to store it while they hibernate. However, most hamsters are strictly solitary and are learning to balance a hermit existence with the need to build a home for a family.

And the females are learning to protect their young in the best way they can. Sometimes they eat them, for they have a very different concept of death from ours. This is only done with permission from Archangel Fhelyai, the angel of animals. At other times they will carry the pups in their cheek pouches to keep them safe.

These little animals can hear and communicate with the angelic and elemental realms. Like many species of animal that live underground they are connected to Archangel Sandalphon, the angel in charge of the Earth Star chakra, and give feedback about what is going on in the earth.

Unusually they also communicate with Archangel Preminilek, the angel in charge of the insects, and tell him what the different species of insect need. If, for example, the soil is too dry for certain insects in the environs of the hamsters the angels will send in the pixies or other elementals to help change the conditions.

Chapter 25

Rhinoceroses

Message from the Rhinoceroses

I love Earth. I love the trees and animals and humans and the feeling of the ground beneath me. I want to stay here.

My service work is very important. If you anchor into Hollow Earth and connect your 12 fifth-dimensional chakras to the stars you too can be a bridge from Source to Lady Gaia and a central point of light for the higher energies of the universe.

Rhinos are fifth-dimensional beings from Lakumay, the ascended aspect of Sirius. It is the fortitude with which they have borne the cruelty of humans that has finally allowed them to ascend fully into the fifth dimension.

There are five species of rhino, three of which are native to Asia – the Indian rhinoceros, Javan rhinoceros and Sumatran rhinoceros – and two native to Africa – the black rhinoceros and the white rhinoceros. They love being on Earth, whether in Africa or Asia, they relish the feel of the land, the trees and the water. As part of their service work the black rhinos agreed to prune trees, while the white rhinos developed different jaws and act as grass mowers.

I remember watching on television a young rhino who had been brought up by humans because its mother had been killed by poachers. This youthful creature was full of joie de vivre, rolling in a muddy puddle and splashing. It could have been a puppy if it had been rather smaller.

These extraordinary animals, the second largest on Earth, are carrying in their energy fields the information, knowledge and wisdom of the Golden Age of Mu, the civilization that preceded Lemuria.

Rhinos, as big heavy animals, are very strongly grounded into Earth itself. They link energetically into Hollow Earth and connect with the healing blue-aquamarine flame of Mother Mary and Archangel Michael, which is held here. With the assistance of Archangels Sandalphon and Roquiel they spread this light, wisdom and healing wherever they walk.

Archangel Sandalphon is seen as black and white, sometimes merging into grey, or when people vibrate at the upper levels of the fifth dimension they see him as shimmering silver. He is in charge of the Earth Star chakras of all creatures and helps them to develop. Individual human and animal Earth Star chakras are their own personal fifth-dimensional paradise, containing the blueprint of their highest potential, where all their wisdom as well as their hope and happiness is stored. Archangel Sandalphon works very closely with Archangel Roquiel, who is a Universal Angel of the Seraphim frequency and is seen as black in colour. He helps people and animals to plug their Earth Star chakras into Lady Gaia to be charged with her light. He also helps individuals' Earth Star and Stellar Gateway chakras to open at the same time.

Rhinoceroses are bridges between Source and Earth. Archangel Roquiel gathers the energy that flows down through these creatures via Archangel Sandalphon. Some of this he directs to Lady Gaia to help the Earth, so that it goes to the portals, ley lines and pyramids. The remaining energy he passes to Orion, Sirius, the Pleiades and Neptune, who are all helping Earth to ascend.

The Universal Metatron Cube

Rhinos do yet more service work for Earth. Imagine Earth as the heart in the centre of a Universal Metatron Cube, surrounded by six circles that are in turn surrounded by six more. These circles represent Sirius, the Seraphim, Orion, Neptune, Roquiel and the Pleiades (*see below*). Lines from the heart of Earth link to the hearts of all the other stars, planets and constellations. In the centre of the heart of Earth is the blue-aquamarine flame of Mary and Michael held by the beings of Mu and the souls of the rhinoceroses. So the rhinoceroses are helping to hold Earth, Orion, Sirius, the Pleiades and Neptune together, so that we can all move together into higher dimensions.

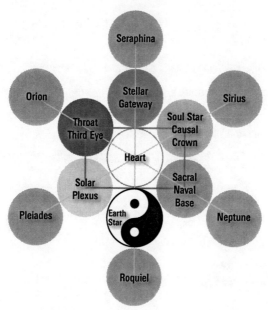

The Universal Metatron Cube

And so as the majestic, ponderous rhinoceroses walk across the plains of Africa and Asia they are spreading the light that is bringing Earth, Orion, Sirius, the Pleiades and Neptune together. They are holding the geometric structure that connects the ascension planets and helping Earth to ascend. The value of their presence on Earth is incalculable. We need them and should be incredibly grateful that they honour us by choosing to incarnate here to serve us.

I was once blessed to see two rhinoceroses, probably mother and daughter, plodding across a hot, dusty plain in Africa. They were heading for a small tree, the only shade available, and once there they circled before settling down, tail to tail, looking in opposite directions, watching out for each other. They felt so belonging, so much part of the landscape, I felt overwhelmed with delight to have seen them.

VISUALIZATION TO HELP THE RHINOCEROSES

1. Find a place where you can be quiet and undisturbed.
2. Visualize yourself sitting in a safe place on a hill overlooking hot parched plains.
3. The flame-red sun is blazing as it starts to set.
4. Be aware of a rhinoceros plodding steadily across the land – quiet, harmless, at one with his surroundings.
5. Notice the stream of energy flowing down towards him from Source.
6. Notice the stream of blue-aquamarine light flowing towards him from the centre of the Earth, lighting him up.
7. Be aware of two vast angelic beings with him; one silver and one black. These are Archangels Sandalphon and Roquiel.

8. You see or sense that the rhinoceros is in the centre of a vast Universal Metatron Cube, holding together the Earth, Orion, Sirius, the Pleiades and Neptune.

9. Thank this awesome creature for his service work.

10. Ask the angel of animals, Archangel Fhelyai, to keep them safe.

Chapter 26

Sheep

Message from the Sheep

Be true to yourself and honour your mission.
Whatever happens to you and no matter what
others do to you, hold your vision. Forgive all those
who harm you. Do this and your soul will be a
radiant light. You will become an Illumined One.

Sheep originally incarnated to offer their services in the time of Golden Atlantis. They arrived from the Pleiades and were the third animal to come from this star cluster, the other two being pigs and pandas.

Their main offering was their wool. Of course the people always asked for permission before they took it. As a result, the sheep gladly gave it and this respectful reciprocation helped to keep everyone's heart open and light. They also gladly shared their milk if it was asked of them.

All creatures from the Pleiades or who step down through that star cluster carry the symbol of a blue rose in their aura. The 33 petals carry the Christ Light of unconditional love and enable them to bear their conditions with fortitude and at the same time to spread love.

Sheep step down into Earth from the Pleiades through the high-frequency portal in Mount Shasta, California, that is in the charge of Archangel Gabriel. Archangel Gabriel and his twin flame Archangel Hope stay connected with the sheep during their lives. In fact, through sheep, Archangel Hope connects to people and touches them with rays of hope, helping to keep spirits high. This enables humanity to aspire to their fullest potential and eventually fulfil their soul destiny.

These delightful animals have a reputation for being stupid but in fact they are heart-centred, intelligent animals. They have learned that when they act together they can be more effective. In the time of Atlantis, the grass was a much higher frequency so their milk and their wool radiated at the perfect frequency that was needed. Woollen clothes would emit a blue healing energy field which would be felt by the wearer.

At that time, they were dancing, happy, frolicking creatures – more like big, woolly lambs than the serious creatures we see these days. They grazed around the houses, helping to keep the grass short so that a rich variety of herbs and wildflowers grew too. The children in the villages would play with them and the sheep really felt belonging and valued. Everyone loved and honoured them.

Like many of the animals who came into the golden era of Atlantis, sheep and rams demonstrated a perfect masculine-feminine balance. Part of their mission was to learn to stay in balance and teach this balance by example. As the animals stayed in yin yang harmony, they would hold the people in balance too.

At that time everything in the human and animal world was done as a perfect exchange. Humans offered sheep love, shelter and extra food if it was needed. Sheep offered humans heart healing, joy, milk and wool in exchange. Everyone was satisfied. All was karmically in tune and alignment.

What used to be a mission of love and faith to Earth has become a challenging sacrifice. Neither the sheep nor any other animal has given permission for their flesh to be consumed by humans nor to be used as sacrificial lambs.

However, even today where there are sheep the blue Angels of the Pleiades can be seen in the meadows amongst them. These glorious angels are supporting the sheep, helping their hearts to stay strong and open. They also help the animals to hold their vision of spreading heart healing to people and into the land. The gentle, forgiving sheep continue to do this even though they know they are going to be slaughtered and eaten.

And because a lamb represents innocence, purity, joy, giving, love and many other beautiful qualities, this is the animal that was offered as a gift of the heart for the baby that was to become the Christ of the age. It also honoured the glowing innocent hearts of the sheep.

VISUALIZATION TO CONNECT WITH THE HEART OF SHEEP

1. Find a place where you can be relaxed and undisturbed.
2. Ask the Angels of the Pleiades to bathe you in their beautiful soft blue light.
3. Breathe this light into your heart.
4. Your guardian angel is presenting you with a soft white lamb. Take it and hold it.
5. Look into its eyes and see the pure glowing innocence of this creature.
6. Feel your own heart opening and expanding as you cuddle it.
7. Sense the love pouring from your own heart to all the sheep in the world.
8. Ask the Angels of the Pleiades to take your love and thanks to every sheep in the world.

9. Sense them all being touched by a blue Angel of the Pleiades, who whispers your message to them.

10. Be aware you have lit a blazing cosmic torch of love and healing in the universe.

11. Return your lamb to your guardian angel.

12. Open your eyes and notice how you feel.

Chapter 27

Squirrels

Message from the Squirrels

*Focus on all the beautiful things around you and see
the best in everything. Enjoy life while you can for in
the great universal scheme of things it is very short and
Earth is a very special place to be. So lighten up!*

Red Squirrels

Beautiful little red squirrels come from Orion. They are no way related spiritually to the grey or black squirrels who come from Sirius and have totally different characters and soul purposes.

The life mission of the red squirrel is very simple. It is to experience life and to spread joy, fun and liveliness to all they see.

I find this very interesting for I remember my grandfather as quite a dour person. However, he found a little red squirrel when he was a boy. He saved its life and looked after it. It survived to become his companion and friend. Apparently the squirrel would wait on a branch of a tree outside the school gates every day, arriving as my grandfather came out of class at the end of lessons. Then it would ride home on his shoulder. To me that's a perfect symbiotic relationship between a very serious child and an animal whose purpose is to lighten people up, so that they see life as a happier place.

Red squirrels carry very fast-frequency cosmic wisdom in their aura. Their service mission is to demonstrate qualities of lightness, joy, freedom, happiness and fun. By tuning in to these delightful little characters you may be touched by their higher qualities. If you are watching a red squirrel it opens you up to its special light. Its soul mission is to offer you enlightenment and you may find yourself seeing things from a higher perspective. They have the ability to help people and other animals to consider information and act on it wisely and lightly.

I was in a park in Hamburg when a red squirrel jumped from a tree, landing in front of me. It pranced about and I was totally enchanted. There was something about that little creature that automatically made me smile and feel happy. They have this quality that enables them to light up people's auras and turn life into something joyful and bright. The red squirrels are heart-centred creatures and they love to open the hearts of people.

Archangel Gabriel works with them. He connects through them to human base chakras to dissolve some of our survival fears and replace them with happiness and joy.

Archangel Mariel, who is in charge of the Soul Star chakra, also works with red squirrels. They help to bring your soul qualities, and therefore your soul mission, forward. If one appears to you it is linking to your energy fields and connecting you with Archangel Mariel, so that your mission can evolve. Until the Cosmic Moment in 2012 Archangel Mariel was not fully present in this universe so the service that the red squirrel offers was deeply important. Since that time, however, because more people have brought in their 12 chakras and many more are ready to do so, Archangel Mariel has stepped fully into our universe and is giving us his focus and attention.

Squirrels

He is helping us all to connect with our soul missions. At the same time red squirrels are becoming rarer and rarer as more people can connect directly with Archangel Mariel.

Grey Squirrels

These highly intelligent little creatures come from Sirius. They are much bigger and heavier than the red squirrels, and more ruthless. They are very inquisitive and highly clever puzzle-solvers. It is part of their mission to develop their brain so that they can accomplish problem-solving. This develops different neural pathways in their brains and they take new information and expanded capabilities back to Sirius at the end of their lives.

Grey squirrels, therefore, are learning about solving physical problems on Earth. They are also teaching humans that there is a solution to problems and if we try hard enough and look at things from different angles we will be able to find new ways of doing them.

Like all beings from Sirius they carry in their energy fields knowledge about spiritual technology and sacred geometry for this universe. When you are ready to receive some of this information a grey squirrel will approach you, possibly without you even being aware of it, and allow you to draw what you need into your own aura. You may say, 'I went for a walk' or 'I sat under a tree and suddenly the solution presented itself to me.'

If there are no grey squirrels in your vicinity another animal from Sirius, who carries the codes that you need, will come to you or pass by you. We live in an amazing universe of interconnected energies. Whenever you are ready you will attract to you what you need.

This bright little animal originally lived in the United States but when its energy was needed in Europe, it was introduced here. It is never by chance that an animal is taken to a different country. There is always a spiritual reason for it. This may be that

165

the energy is required to trigger a change or that it is teaching lessons. In the case of the grey squirrel, when we allowed it to decimate the indigenous red squirrel population, we were being taught that it is important to look after and cherish what we have. But it was also time for the grey squirrel to wake up news of spiritual technology within the consciousness of people here.

The grey squirrel also has a wonderful sense of fun. It loves to play games, chasing its friends up and down trees. Equally it loves to be presented with a problem. The challenge of getting at food is irresistible.

They have driven my little dog, Venus, to distraction on occasions when they have jumped to the ground in front of her, run across a space just wide enough that she can't catch them, climbed the next tree and then jumped down again to repeat the loop. Another favourite is for a squirrel to wait for her to come along a path by a fence. At the optimum moment the squirrel races along the fence while the dog chases along the ground barking. At the far end it leaps, light as a feather, into a branch. Grey squirrels are definitely teases! And making people laugh is part of their service.

Because we live on a planet with gravity, every creature has to find a way of handling it. In the golden era of Atlantis, the High Priests and Priestesses and Magi learned how to overcome gravity and could levitate or fly by activating their kundalini. Kangaroos, monkeys, spiders and other creatures are learning to use their kundalini in a variety of ways. All squirrels are learning and teaching about a different use of kundalini. By working with their tail and their vital force they can leap across incredible distances for their size. Using their tails correctly they bound and leap and almost fly. This is another skill they are honing to take back to Sirius.

Grey squirrels are connected with the great Master Hilarion, Master of the Fifth Ray, who works with science and technology and is helping to bring forward the spiritual technology for the new Golden Age starting in 2032. They are also very connected to Archangel Raphael, who is in charge of the development of the third eye of all sentient beings. Archangel Raphael is also the angel of healing and abundance. However, this archangel works with grey squirrels mostly because of the sacred geometry they carry in their third eye.

Black Squirrels

Black squirrels are also third-dimensional animals from Sirius. In their case, black does not denote the divine feminine but rather aggressive force. They carry much more testosterone than grey squirrels. They are bigger, faster, and more fiercely territorial than the grey ones and are showing us that masculine domination through aggression is not the way forward for a happy, balanced society. Humans can watch how the black squirrels have spread simply by using their masculine power, but this does not bring peace or harmony into the squirrel population.

The animal kingdom is constantly teaching us. The grey and black squirrels are teaching us of the dangers of allowing the masculine dominance to overpower us.

Animals come to Earth to learn and teach. Black squirrels are learning about an imbalance of masculine-feminine energy and this is also what they are teaching humans. They are bringing us a message about what happens when masculine energy dominates. Because they are demonstrating such an important lesson to us, Archangel Metatron is watching over the black squirrels. He connects people through the Stellar Gateway chakra to Mars and eventually to its ascended aspect Nigellay. Mars is the masculine-dominant planet of war and aggression. Nigellay represents the ascended masculine, the peaceful warrior, the bringer of good leadership and peace.

As we observe the black squirrel we can take a decision individually and collectively to balance the masculine with feminine wisdom and allow peace to spread through Earth.

VISUALIZATION TO MEET THE SQUIRRELS

1. Find a place where you can be quiet and undisturbed.

2. Ask Archangel Michael to place his royal-blue cloak around you, lighting you up and protecting you.

3. Find yourself sitting in a sunny glade. All is peaceful and still.

4. You see a bright emerald light appearing on one side of the glade. As it approaches you see it is Archangel Raphael. With him bounds a little grey squirrel.

5. They stand on your right-hand side.

6. And then Archangel Gabriel in a shimmering diamond-white light approaches with a tiny joy-filled red squirrel, hopping along beside him.

7. They stand on your left-hand side.

8. Imagine you can see the aura of the grey squirrel, with its sacred geometric shapes and keys and code of knowledge from Sirius.

9. Then have a sense of the gentle rainbow aura of the red squirrel, filled with joie de vivre, fun and light and the wisdom of Orion.

10. Archangel Raphael is linking the energy field of the grey squirrel into your third eye. Relax and experience what this feels like and what you receive.

11. Archangel Gabriel is now linking the energy field of the red squirrel into your base chakra. Relax and experience what this feels like and what you receive.

12. With a sense of their gifts and talents, their purpose and their characters, send each of them love.

13. Then thank them for what they have each given you and open your eyes.

PART III
~

AQUATIC CREATURES

Chapter 1

Dolphins

Message from the Dolphins

Live joyfully in the present. The only important time is now, and your current thoughts and actions create your future. Have fun, play and relax so that the knowledge and information coded in your cells can easily be released. Then you will be a wise one.

Dolphins are fifth-dimensional beings with a seventh-dimensional blueprint, who originate from Lakumay, the ascended aspect of Sirius. They carry the sacred geometric codes of light from the highest-frequency time of Golden Atlantis, with the result that many entities have tried to destroy them in order to access the information. Not only do the dolphins hold the keys of the knowledge and wisdom of that time but they express them with joy and lightness. They pass the information into the waters of the oceans and rivers so that creatures swimming in their vicinity can receive it.

They are practising and teaching echolocation and sonic purification. In addition, the Gold Ray of Christ is held in Lakumay and the dolphins are now channelling this through their energy fields at a ninth-dimensional frequency to allow it to light up the waters with the codes of higher love.

Because dolphins are so important, an army of highly evolved sea creatures protects them; the sharks, the whales, the rays and the turtles.

All dolphins are great healers and there are many recorded stories of healings they have performed. Usually, they raise the frequency of the emotional or mental body of the afflicted, and this very quickly translates into healing the physical.

Many dolphins have not always been high-frequency aquatic beings. Some were those humans with enormous amounts of technological knowledge who caused the fall of Atlantis by using it for selfish purposes. At the end of that era they were given a choice. They knew that if they reincarnated on Earth they could cause untold damage and create much more karma for themselves. So, very unusually, the Intergalactic Council offered them the opportunity to take dolphin bodies, which would hold the sacred geometry of the Atlantean crystal technology. In the oceans they could not use the power this gave them to inflict harm. Instead they could work off their karma by spreading the spiritual information into the waters. At the same time the sacred geometry they hold creates sonics that purify the oceans wherever they swim.

Because dolphins are mammals they would have the opportunity of giving birth to live young and caring for and nurturing their offspring. It was felt that this would help to hold their hearts open. Water carries the love energy of the universe and this too would help them to open their hearts and clear their karma more quickly. They agreed to this opportunity for redemption.

This karma was finally repaid by 2012 and all dolphins are now spreading pure light.

In addition, many of the Angels of Atlantis were offered an unusual opportunity to experience physical existence. They too took dolphin bodies and swam in the oceans in order to keep an eye on the other dolphins. The angel dolphins radiate an electric-blue aura which is visible to humans. They are also great healers and transmuters of energy.

Despite the way they may have misused their knowledge in the past, all dolphins are highly evolved beings. No dolphin allows itself to be caught in a net or beaches itself unless its soul allows it. They do so in order to awaken humanity to the pollution in the oceans or the cruelty of our fishing methods. They are trying to open the hearts of people with compassion. They are endeavouring to make us aware of what we are doing to our beautiful planet.

At the same time, they are learning about cooperating with each other and helping each other for the highest good by living in heart-centred social pods.

Like all ocean creatures, dolphins connect very closely with Archangel Joules, who has his retreat in the centre of the Bermuda Triangle where the Great Crystal of Atlantis fell. The Bermuda Triangle is a cosmic portal that started to open on a permanent basis in 2012. The centre of the Bermuda Triangle is an energetic meeting point for seventh-dimensional energy flowing down from Source and up from Hollow Earth. It holds the seventh-dimensional blueprint of the waters and spreads this to the ocean creatures in order to assist their ascension.

Through this portal the dolphins connect into Hollow Earth and provide a two-way communication with Lady Gaia.

VISUALIZATION TO CONNECT WITH THE DOLPHINS

1. Find a place where you can be quiet and undisturbed. It is special if you can do this visualization while lying in the bath or even floating in a warm sea.

2. Ask a beautiful Angel of Atlantis to place its wings gently around you and let yourself sink into the soft energy as you relax.

3. Be aware of glorious warm blue sea and sky around you.

4. As you float safely in the ocean be aware of a silver dolphin arcing through the waters towards you.

5. Its aura is a bright electric-blue which reflects on the ripples. In front of it pours a stream of sacred geometric keys and codes and you can see them light up and purify the waters.

6. All at once the water feels lighter and you can see the sacred symbols form around you.

7. Breathe in deeply. Take in the wisdom of Atlantis. Allow it to be downloaded into your cells.

8. And now play lightly and joyfully with the dolphin. Ride on its back and splash in the water. Have fun.

9. Feel the electric-blue healing energy flowing round your mental and emotional bodies soothing and healing you, then pouring through your physical body, healing you at a cellular level.

10. Open yourself up to the Gold Ray of Christ that is pouring through the dolphin's energy fields and enveloping you with love and higher wisdom.

11. As you and the dolphin leap and surge through the ocean know that you are purifying the ocean and leaving a trail of healing, wisdom and love.

12. When it is time to finish your ride, thank the dolphin and watch it swimming away.

13. Find yourself back where you started.

Chapter 2

~

Frogs and Toads

Message from the Frogs and Toads

Water is the most amazing element. It carries cosmic love and the power of physical and soul purification. We urge you to spend more time in water. Love it, bless it and thank it. Bathing, swimming, showering or walking in the rain accelerates your ascension and fills your heart with more love.

Frogs

Frogs live mostly in the water and have to be near it in order to lay their spawn in it. Because they spend so much time in the water element their energy is pure. They are very connected to the water elementals, the undines.

Their service work is to keep insects and slugs and snails under control when they become too numerous.

Most frogs are third-dimensional and leave their mates as soon as the frogspawn is laid. Some types of frog are moving into the fourth dimension and care for their offspring by keeping the spawn safe in a pouch until they hatch. A few male frogs stay around and watch over the frogspawn during incubation but this is rare. They are also social creatures and live in groups. Often groups of young frogs swim together much like fish.

Frogs jump huge distances for their size. They are teaching and learning about different ways of using their kundalini energy as well as the power of their legs. Depending on their habitat and their needs some can jump high, others a long distance.

They originate from Neptune, the planet of higher spirituality, and their soul mission is to bring in universal wisdom and light and spread it. They also connect with Hollow Earth, though not like reptiles who are on the ground. However, frogs are able to bring up some of the seventh-dimensional light from Hollow Earth and spread it wherever they go at the same time as they spread universal wisdom.

When people are asleep they keep their spiritual connections open. This is a time of spiritual sustenance and renewal. Because frogs hibernate when it freezes they spend this time in connection with the wisdom of their home planet. This helps to keep them spiritually aligned.

Archangel Michael works with the highly developed throat chakras of frogs. The croaking and other sounds they utter are a way of communication, calling to prospective mates, warning and also sending out healing messages into the universe. Their sounds cleanse, purify and raise the frequency of the area. In all creatures the throat chakra governs the thyroid gland. Frogs are constantly receiving and emitting messages so that their throat chakras are very stimulated and this is implicit in the bulging eyes of the frog. In addition, it is hormones released from the tadpole's thyroid gland that trigger the metamorphosis from tadpole into a frog. Like butterflies, frogs demonstrate that it is possible to transform completely!

Like all water-based creatures, frogs are very connected to Archangel Joules and it is through his energy that they can link to Hollow Earth.

VISUALIZATION TO CONNECT WITH THE FROGS

1. Find a place where you can be quiet and undisturbed.
2. Breathe deeply and let yourself relax more on each outbreath.
3. Imagine or sense yourself sitting by a pond on a still, warm moonlit night.
4. As you listen to the sound of frogs croaking all around you, you feel one with the frog kingdom.
5. A beautiful pale pink light rises from the water and the frogs, like a mist.
6. Their sounds flows over and through you, purifying, cleansing and healing you. Relax and enjoy this.
7. As this happens sense or see the auras of the trees and rushes lighting up in response.
8. Your aura is also lighting up and you become a radiant pink beacon of love.
9. You are connecting to the love energy of the water through your link to the frog kingdom.
10. Thank the frogs and bless them for their wonderful soul work!

Toads

Toads have a similar spiritual mission to frogs. Like frogs they are amphibians. They live on land but always fairly near water and they mate in or by a sluggish stream or pond. Their spawn needs to be in water and some toads put the string of spawn on their back and make sure it reaches the right place. They too hibernate during the winter but are more land-based so they hide in deep leaf litter, log piles and in burrows.

Tadpoles hatch from the spawn after about ten days and they gradually change completely, or metamorphose, into toadlets over about two months. Their soul mission is to demonstrate that it is possible to change utterly and completely.

The service mission of the toads is the same as for frogs; to keep insects and slugs and snails under control when they become too numerous.

They also originate from Neptune but are not as high frequency as frogs because they do not have such a close relationship with water.

Chapter 3

Fish and Shellfish

Message from the Fish and Shellfish

Every creature in the universe is connected through the cosmic love flowing in water. We are particularly blessed because we are bathed in water all the time. When you think about us you automatically draw the love and divine harmony of the universe to you. We are messengers of oneness.

Fish are third- to fifth-dimensional beings. Most small fish are third-dimensional and belong to a group soul of thousands while some of the larger fish, like trout or even cod, belong to a group soul of hundreds. Individualized fish are fifth-dimensional. All are on their ascension pathway like every other sentient being in the universe and are doing their part to help the planet.

Their service mission is to keep the seas and oceans clean and clear both physically and spiritually. They eat the detritus but they also bring in the sonics of the angels and so help to keep the waters at a high vibration.

The soul mission of all ocean creatures is to experience life in a physical body – to enjoy the feel of the waters and the sun and wind, to learn about taste and even smell. And most importantly to be in touch with the cosmic love energy held in the water. This helps their ascension process.

Those that are part of a group soul are learning to work and react together and to move in harmony and cooperation with others. This happens when their hearts are open because a heart connection enables psychic abilities to develop.

They are helped by the undines, who are water elementals, and also by mermaids who look after the plants in the oceans.

The ocean kingdom is in the care of the mighty blue-green Universal Angel Joules, and he oversees the lives of the fish. Most fish come from the constellation Pisces and step down to Earth through Neptune. Because Neptune holds the spiritual wisdom of the universe, those creatures who step down through here bring some of that wisdom with them in their energy fields. This then spreads into the waters.

All ocean creatures are connected to the moon and bring the divine feminine light down through the waters. This is helping to balance the masculine-feminine qualities on the planet. It also enables fish, animals and humans to open up psychically and spiritually for all water is connected. The water you drink is connected energetically to the water in the sea. Since 2015, the year of the super moons, this process has accelerated.

Our oceans and waterways are vast and carry the love of the universe, so the seas and oceans are huge receptacles for this frequency. Aeons ago it became obvious to the Intergalactic Council that an army of volunteers would be needed to keep this enormous, important area of Earth clear and cleansed.

Many group souls from throughout the universes offered to come to Earth to eat the decaying organic matter, including dead animals that would otherwise pollute the seas. In exchange they would take back to their home planet experiences and information about Earth.

As humans polluted Earth more and more it became obvious that the volunteers could no longer cope. Again a call went out into the universes for assistance. Elementals called kyhils offered to come to Earth to try to consume the toxins that the fish could no longer deal with. These tiny elementals even ingest the oil pollution that has been created.

Lobsters, langoustines, prawns, shrimp and crabs scuttle around eating fresh food when they can but they also do a heroic job scavenging for dead animals on the sea floor and so keeping it clear. They are the vultures of the ocean world.

Oysters, clams, cockles, whelks, winkles and mussels similarly consume decaying organic matter that sinks to the sea floor, including sewage. They are the beetles and cockroaches of the ocean world. So too are cuttlefish, octopus and squid. Sea urchins mainly feed on algae on the coral and rocks and also consume decomposing matter such as dead fish, mussels, sponges and barnacles. For thousands of years they have done their part to help us all.

Seahorses are particularly beloved fish, partly because of their unique horse-like shape and also because of their interesting life choices. Their oversoul has chosen a unique experience in the oceans. A male and female mate for life. Early each morning they meet their partner where their individual territories overlap and reinforce their bonding with an elaborate courtship display. As they meet they change colour and the male then circles around the female. Then they often spiral around an object before the female returns to her own territory. They both change colour frequently to blend in with their surroundings.

They are learning about masculine and feminine roles and for this purpose the female transfers her eggs to the male which he then fertilizes himself in a pouch. Here everything they need is provided until the fry hatch and are born live, about 1cm long, after a long birthing process which can last up to twelve hours.

They are learning and teaching about loyalty, love, keeping romance alive, the art of blending in with your surroundings and understanding masculine and feminine energy.

Surprising for a creature that has decided to live in the waters, seahorses are poor swimmers. They rely on their prehensile tail which allows them to grip onto weeds so that they are not washed away by tides and currents.

Like other fish their service mission is to keep the oceans clean and clear while their soul mission is to demonstrate love and loyalty.

Fish of the Coral Reefs

All the amazing brightly coloured fish that dart about on the coral reefs are fifth-dimensional, for where there is living coral the frequencies are very high. Coral reefs are receiving and transmitting stations for the oceans. They communicate with the ancient wisdom of Hollow Earth and then send back information about the ocean, what it needs and how those who live in it are progressing spiritually.

The coral reefs are also entrusted to spread hope and optimism throughout the oceans. Because all waters are connected they are doing this for the world.

VISUALIZATION TO CONNECT WITH THE FISH

1. If possible fill a glass with cold pure water and sip it.
2. Find a place where you can be quiet and undisturbed.
3. Close your eyes and relax.
4. You are aware of the beautiful blue-green light of Archangel Joules watching and protecting you.

5. Visualize yourself floating in a warm sea on a moonlit night, relaxed and safe.

6. A shoal of small fish swim round you. They are bringing you a message of love and peace and joy. Breathe it in.

7. They remind you that when you work and cooperate with others your heart opens and you develop telepathy and empathy.

8. Send love to these fish as you watch them swim away together.

9. Open your eyes and drink the rest of your water knowing all creatures are one.

Chapter 4

~

Rays

Message from the Rays

We are the fish angels of the oceans, ambassadors from the Pleiades. When you think of us we link you energetically to the Pleiades so that you receive a download of healing energy.

We invite you to connect with us so that together we can heal your beautiful oceans and raise the frequency of the waters of your planet. We send you greetings and love.

Rays are beautiful fifth-dimensional creatures from the Pleiades. All beings who originate from here are dedicated healers no matter what shape or form they take on Earth.

The rays carry the blue healing light of the Pleiades in their auras and spread it over the waters and to all ocean creatures. They work closely with the blue Angels of the Pleiades, who direct them to go where they are needed.

Pleiadean healing is sent from the heart and heals through the hearts of the recipients. As beings open and develop their heart centres, etheric wings form. Wings are the visible expansion of love energy radiating out. In the case of birds and rays these wings have become physical.

So these wonderful fish with radiant glowing hearts raise the frequency of the oceans by pouring heart-healing energy wherever they go. Even the small skates do their part. Their soul mission and their service work is the same, to spread healing and love as they undulate with beauty, grace and elegance through the oceans.

The rays form part of the network to protect the information and wisdom held by the dolphins. Their task is to raise the frequency of the water and all the fish around the dolphins so that the lower energies cannot penetrate the auras of the great ones.

They also work with Archangel Joules and link through the cosmic portal of Lemuria into the Great Pyramid of Hollow Earth to bring up and spread Lemurian knowledge.

Like most fish their energy is amplified at the full moon when they link into lunar light and are bathed in divine feminine energy. At that time their auras become pearlescent blue and are wondrous to see.

Visualization to Work with the Rays

Before you start this visualization you might like to get a glass of pure water, bless it and thank it and ask the Angels of the Pleiades to fill it with healing blue light.

1. Find a place where you can be quiet and undisturbed.

2. Close your eyes and let yourself relax.

3. Find yourself lying on soft cushions on the deck of an elegant yacht, watching the pearly moon floating in the sky.

4. Feel the gentle, rocking movement of the boat and listen to the sound of the waves.

5. Become aware of a huge ray with a glorious blue aura undulating through the water towards you.

6. As the blue healing light surrounds you breathe it into your heart.

7. Seamlessly, you find yourself sitting safe and secure on the ray's back.

8. Looking up, you see a blue shaft of light reaching all the way up to the Pleiades and beautiful blue angels surround you.

9. You and the ray are held in a vast orb of blue as you fly and float through the oceans.

10. When you move through shoals of fish, they all light up and you know you have made a difference.

11. You float together over a coral reef and the entire reef blazes with healing light.

12. And suddenly the ray receives a call for help. An angel dolphin is entering an area of the ocean where the energy is dense.

13. You hold tight as the ray flies faster through the waters. Around you are sharks, whales and turtles, all racing in the same direction to help.

14. You invoke Archangel Joules and his angels and in a flash you are all pouring high-frequency green-blue light into the waters round the brave dolphin.

15. The waters light up. The density is dispersed. The sharks, turtles, whales and dolphin nod their thanks to you and the ray.

16. You find yourself once more lying on the soft cushions on the deck of the yacht.

17. Take a few moments to enjoy the good feeling of knowing you and the rays have helped the entire ocean kingdom.

18. Open your eyes and sip the water full of the blue healing light from the Pleiades.

Chapter 5

~

Sharks

Message from the Sharks

*When you think about us we remind you to stand in your power
with discipline but in a gentle and harmonious way. Respect
all creatures whoever they are and whatever their reputation.
And finally carry the diamond of love in your heart and beam
it out to connect beings throughout the universe with love.*

Many people are surprised to discover that sharks are fifth-dimensional. They originate from the ascended aspect of Mars, called Nigellay. While humans tend to see their martial aspect, in fact they also carry in their aura the qualities of the wise and powerful leader, the spiritual warrior, protecting those less capable of looking after themselves than they are.

Their soul mission is to patrol the oceans keeping things in divine right order. They stand no nonsense and expect discipline. Like martial-arts experts, in their own world they have a code of ethics. They practise and teach respect, honour and focus.

Sharks form part of the spiritual army of sea creatures who protect the wisdom held by the dolphins. They are formidable in the pursuance of their duty.

Their service mission is to scavenge and keep the oceans clear and clean.

Sharks have a very powerful sense of smell and can taste, touch, see and hear. They are also incredibly psychic with a well-developed third eye. They can sense tiny movements and vibrations in the water and know exactly where the activity is.

Over 90 per cent of the large sharks of the world have already been killed by humans. So why would the oversoul of such evolved creatures allow this to happen? As with many endangered species they have sacrificed themselves in order to draw our attention to what is happening in our oceans. They want us to see how very important they are to maintaining the ecosystems of the waters of this planet. The question is, will humanity become enlightened before it is too late?

Sharks have long engendered fear in people and certain horror films about them have given them an undeserved reputation. It is time to respect them for who they truly are – great spiritual warriors of the oceans.

Any creature who comes from Mars or its ascended aspect Nigellay has a link with Archangel Metatron. That mighty archangel is in charge of the development of the Stellar Gateway chakra of all creatures. The Stellar Gateway chakra of the universe is Mars\Nigellay. The Stellar Gateway chakra is like a great golden-orange chalice. Archangel Metatron keeps this chakra in fifth-dimensional creatures open and pours universal light into it. Sharks help all fifth-dimensional ocean beings to link with Archangel Metatron and keep their Stellar Gateways open. They also radiate the keys and codes of ascension into the waters to accelerate the paths of all sea creatures and help guide them to their ascension path.

We tend to think of sharks as masculine-dominant and aggressive. In fact, they have balanced their masculine and feminine energies on their paths to becoming spiritual peace warriors. At the opening of the Lyran Stargate at the super moon of September 2015 huge numbers of beings, animal, fish and human, opened their hearts in a way that allowed them to move from the golden ascension path to the diamond path, which is a much higher frequency. Amongst them were the sharks, and their higher diamond-light codes have been activated. This enables them to connect more strongly to their planet of origin and also send their light out to other parts of the universe. They are now diamond sparks in the multiverse.

Archangel Joules, the archangel of the waters, is also working with sharks. He uses their light to beam information and wisdom from and about the waters of Earth to other star systems, to enable our universe to ascend more quickly.

VISUALIZATION TO CONNECT WITH THE SHARKS

1. Find a place where you can be quiet and undisturbed.

2. Archangel Joules is placing a blue-green mantle of light and protection around you.

3. You find yourself floating in blue-green waters, feeling totally safe, calm and relaxed as you watch the stars.

4. Your heart is open and a diamond of light is shining from it connecting with like energy.

5. You are aware of a beautiful, high-frequency shark approaching you, its heart also radiating a diamond of light. You feel utterly safe and protected.

6. The shark circles round you and your 12 chakras light up.

7. Your Stellar Gateway beams out a link through Mars to its ascended aspect Nigellay.

8. At the same time the shark beams out a link through Mars to its ascended aspect Nigellay.

9. A huge burst of diamond light flows down the links into both your hearts.

10. You and the shark are held in a huge cosmic diamond of purity and love.

11. Feel yourself one with the shark and all creatures.

12. Gradually return to where you started and thank the shark and the archangels for the gift of oneness you hold in your energy fields.

Chapter 6

~

Turtles

Message from the Turtles

You live in a beautiful world and your oceans are unparalleled throughout the universes. Our message to you is to cherish their diversity and purity. Each ocean is a vast reservoir of cosmic love and we feel blessed to live in them. All water is connected, so every time you drink a glassful or shower or bathe, bless and thank it. In this way you can help us, the turtles, and the entire universe by raising the frequency and spreading cosmic abundance.

Turtles are highly evolved beings from another universe who step down through the ascended aspect of Jupiter, called Jumbay, in order to help raise and maintain the frequency of our oceans. Until the Cosmic Moment they had to step their energies down through Neptune. However, since 2012 they come in directly via Jupiter, so the light they bring in is purer and clearer.

Jupiter is the planet of happiness, abundance and cosmic joy, and the turtles carry all these energies in their energy fields. Wherever they go they radiate these qualities onto land and into the oceans.

They originally connected with Earth in Lemuria and like all etheric Lemurian beings really love the earth, the waters and everything on the planet.

When a human opens and activates their third eye at a fifth-dimensional frequency under the direction of Archangel Raphael, they can link to Jupiter and Jumbay. Here they can access all levels of cosmic abundance, including prosperity, enlightenment, happiness, peace, love and higher knowing. The turtles also help to facilitate this for the whole of humanity.

When enough people have opened their fifth-dimensional chakras the turtles will be able to bring forward part of their soul mission which is to raise the abundance consciousness of humanity.

All marine creatures are linked to the moon, including the gentle turtles. They bring in divine feminine qualities and lunar wisdom which they spread to fish, animals and humans. They are solid and dependable and can be relied on. This is why they were entrusted with a great soul mission.

Even though they lay eggs and do not carry live young part of their soul mission is to help bring the planet into perfect masculine and feminine balance for the new Golden Age.

Turtles are totally pure and still maintain their original divine blueprint from Source. They carry the innocence of this in their energy fields and those who tune in to them are able to access Source light more easily. This applies to huge turtles but even tiny ones are doing what they can.

They connect to the seventh-dimensional energy of Hollow Earth through the great archangel of the waters, Archangel Joules. They bring up the seventh-dimensional wisdom from the Bermuda Triangle portal and spread it into the waters.

Turtles' shells are designed to protect them physically and also energetically. The shell fends off lower energies and is needed because the turtle is excessively sensitive. They feel, sense and psychically tune in to everything.

Again and again they have sacrificed themselves to help Earth. Because they are highly attuned fifth-dimensional beings they would never eat polythene bags thinking they are jellyfish. No! They go through horrible deaths after eating polythene bags to draw our attention to what we are doing to our planet and particularly our oceans. That is the level of their service and their love of Earth.

An important part of their soul mission is to protect the dolphins, who hold the wisdom of Atlantis and Lemuria in their energy fields. It is vitally important that this sacred and special information is maintained until we are ready to access it and use it for the betterment of the world. Turtles work with the whales, sharks and rays to patrol the oceans to ensure the dolphins are safe. They also raise the frequency of the waters round the dolphins to create an impenetrable wall of light so that lower entities cannot access the information held by the dolphins.

They are totally at one with the ocean and the land. When they lay their eggs on land and leave them there, they are demonstrating trust. They are in tune with the oceans, the currents, the moon and the whole natural world. They radiate this understanding wherever they are.

VISUALIZATION TO CONNECT WITH THE TURTLES

1. Find a place where you can be quiet and undisturbed.

2. Ask the mighty Archangel Joules, archangel of the oceans, to place his blue-green light around you to protect you.

3. Imagine yourself floating in the soft, warm, calm blue waters off Hawaii. Feel all your troubles ebbing away.

4. A huge turtle is moving towards you, peacefully paddling through the waters.

5. The turtle invites you to sit on its back. It slips under you and lifts you up onto its shell. You feel relaxed and safe.

6. And now the turtle is gliding down into the ocean, moving with the currents.

7. It takes you into a glorious coral reef, where fish and mermaids surround you. You realize how honoured and revered it is in the ocean world.

8. The turtle takes you to the Bermuda Triangle, the vast portal where the Great Crystal of Atlantis lies.

9. You touch the Great Crystal and an electric vibration goes through you.

10. A stream of light shoots up from you to Jupiter and then to Jumbay, its ascended aspect.

11. The light then pours back over you and the turtle, filling you with the cosmic abundance of Jupiter and Jumbay.

12. Together you and the turtle float in a leisurely way through the blue oceans spreading the higher light.

13. At last the turtle brings you back to the pure white sand of Hawaii. Thank it and return to where you started.

Chapter 7

Whales

Message from the Whales

*When you think of us our energy automatically connects you
to the divine feminine love healing and wisdom of Angel Mary
and to the wondrous love and light of the Archangel Joules.
Take a moment to rest in the cocoon of blue they form around
you and let them illuminate you through us. We are here
to spread universal love and you are ready to receive it.*

People talk of whales with a sense of awe that is well justified.
They originate from an asteroid in the tenth-dimensional
universe of Shekinah. This is a plane of high-frequency light and
the whales carry within their energy fields the light keys and
codes of pure love and joy that is beyond our understanding.

It is a huge undertaking for their souls to step down
through the dimensions into a physical body in a much lower-
frequency universe like ours. However, whales have done so
for millions of years. Their soul mission has always been to try
to maintain the vibration of our planet and to hold the divine
blueprint for our oceans.

There is a diverse range of whales but the gentle, all-loving
blue whale carries the essence of their soul mission.

The blue whale is the largest-known mammal that has ever lived. It can be up to 34 metres long and weigh 150 tons. All those years ago the Intergalactic Council decided that this high-frequency creature, carrying the essence of love within its physical body and auric fields, would have to be enormous to survive at that time and it would have to live in water. This is because water carries the love energy of the universes and enables creatures living in it to remain pure and uncontaminated by what is happening on the land.

For their part whales wanted to understand the close love that can only be experienced by carrying a living, breathing baby in the womb and giving birth to it. A new model was designed for them and other creatures followed.

From the start whales were bathed in the light of the wondrous Angel Mary, who is a Universal Angel and spreads her divine feminine love throughout the universes. Mary's name is derived from mare, meaning water, and she has a symbiotic relationship with that element. She pours her aquamarine light into the seas, oceans and all waters. When you ask the Angel Mary to bless water, whether it is a glassful you are to drink or a bath or the sea, her blessing raises the frequency to the fifth dimension and it profoundly affects you, mentally, emotionally and at a cellular level. Because of their connection with the Angel Mary, the whales constantly call in her blessings and spread divine feminine wisdom into the waters wherever they swim.

While Archangels vibrate between the seventh and ninth dimension, they can easily reach up into the tenth and eleventh dimensions and even into the twelfth dimension to touch Source energy. Because of this, when you think about whales, swim with them or listen to their sounds the Angel Mary can take you up to ineffable heights that enables your heart to be touched by Source.

The sonar of the whales is more than a communication and incredible echolocation device. It also spreads the light, containing codes of higher enlightenment, and the hope they bring from Shekinah into the waters.

These high-frequency mammals, like monkeys and dolphins, cannot be caught, trapped or killed unless they allow it. They will only sacrifice themselves in order to touch the hearts or minds of humanity with compassion.

Like all marine creatures, whales are very connected with Archangel Joules, who is in charge of the oceans.

As I was writing this, I was clairvoyantly shown a picture of whales gathering in the Bermuda Triangle portal. Angel Mary's aquamarine light was pouring down onto them and Archangel Joules's blue light was shining up through them, so that they were in the centre of a column of love, healing and joy that reached up to Source. This energy was then radiating out into the ocean and millions of creatures were being touched by it.

This blessing was raising the frequency of the waters, which were in turn lapping onto the shores of land masses and lifting the vibration of the Earth.

After I was shown this image I looked at the Internet to see if whales did go to the Bermuda Triangle and discovered that the area was being turned into a protected area for whales, who were gathering there. It was so encouraging to realize that, at some levels, humans really are listening!

Another aspect of the service mission of the whales is to be part of the army protecting the dolphins and the sacred wisdom they hold.

Mastery involves taking responsibility for everything in your life so that you always stand in your power. One of the first steps for a human is to be able to control your breathing. In wiser times, after a shock a Master was expected to return to equilibrium in three breaths.

When we breathe, we unconsciously take in Source energy, for breath is our connection to Source. Whales need to breathe air by coming to the surface of the water. This means they decide consciously when to breathe and this allows them to be consciously connected to Source and their place of origin.

Before you start the visualization to support the soul mission of the whales, take a few moments to think about these beautiful creatures.

VISUALIZATION TO SUPPORT THE SOUL MISSION OF THE WHALES

1. Find a place where you can be quiet and undisturbed.

2. Picture, sense or feel yourself floating in warm, calm, safe waters in the Bermuda Triangle. Relax and surrender.

3. Know that the energy from the Great Crystal of Atlantis below you is supporting you and lighting up the keys and codes of ancient wisdom and knowledge in your aura.

4. Be aware of whales gently and lovingly approaching you, keeping you safe as they swim round you.

5. A column of blue-green light from Archangel Joules rises up from Hollow Earth and surrounds you. You are floating in the wisdom of the universe held in the ocean kingdom.

6. And a column of pure aquamarine light, sent down from the Universal Angel Mary, bathes you in divine feminine love.

7. The blue-green and the aquamarine merge and you are cocooned in glorious high-frequency blue light of ineffable love.

8. You know love is the most important thing in the universes. You soak it in.

9. The light gradually withdraws and the whales are sending you thanks. Thank them in turn.

10. Then find yourself back where you started, smiling at the serendipity of the universe.

PART IV

REPTILES

Chapter 1

Crocodiles and Alligators

Message from the Crocodiles and Alligators

We may not have an emotional body but we do have a spiritual body as well as a pure Source connection. We perform important spiritual work in a cosmic capacity. Our message to you is, 'Do not judge by the outer or even by behaviour.' Look beyond the obvious at the soul of a creature and there you will find the truth of who they are.

Crocodiles and alligators were amongst the first reptiles to come to Earth and still carry the original divine blueprint bestowed on them by Source. Within this they carry pure Source energy. Because of this they know exactly who they are and why they are on Earth. They act according to their innate instincts. These intelligent reptiles coordinate their actions to hunt in groups and communicate telepathically with each other.

They come from other universes. To humans, many creatures from different parts of the unknown cosmos have a strangeness about them and are consequently feared. Like all reptiles they step their energy down through Neptune, which is a watery planet of higher spirituality and psychic awareness.

They also step down through this particular planet because it keeps the wisdom of Atlantis and Lemuria, in order to familiarize themselves with the high-frequency wisdom of those two golden civilizations. They are particularly holding and radiating the ancient wisdom of Lemuria. Their service work is to absorb this wisdom into their energy fields and spread it wherever they go. They spread the keys of Lemurian wisdom beyond Australia to Africa, America and Asia. When you see a basking crocodile it may be working its hardest radiating out the keys and codes of Lemurian wisdom energetically into the world.

They also have a strong connection to Hollow Earth and bring up the knowledge and wisdom of many of the ancient tribes and cultures, then pour it from their energy fields into the land, the trees and any creature who will accept it. In this way they are keeping the history and wisdom of the prehistoric world alive. By spreading the wisdom of Hollow Earth, they help to hold the world steady.

They also connect directly with their home planets and access wisdom from here to pass into Hollow Earth, thus building up the knowledge base of Gaia.

They were on Earth during the Golden Age of Petranium which was the Golden Age of Africa, aeons ago before Mu, Lemuria and Atlantis.

Physically crocodiles have a v-shaped, pointed snout and teeth that stick up over the upper lip, so they look like they are grinning. They are much bigger than alligators, who have wider, u-shaped snouts. The original blueprint designed by Source allowed for these variations as part of different experiments on Earth, to see how each fared on Earth.

These creatures do not have an angel but they are protected and assisted by the elemental kingdom. Because crocodiles and alligators live in water and also crawl or run on the land, both the earth and water elementals work with them.

Undines are third-dimensional water elementals, whose task is to keep water physically and energetically clear. They clear lower energies round these creatures. In exchange these fearsome reptiles pass ancient wisdom and knowledge to the undines, who are delighted to store it and take it back to their planet of origin.

Of the earth elementals elves, pixies and imps have specific roles but the great open-hearted fifth-dimensional goblins are always willing to assist them. They help to coordinate the movements of the crocodiles and alligators so that the wisdom they carry is spread where it can be best used. They also endeavour to help the reptiles to see things from a higher perspective.

Dragons too are elementals. They may have one element or two or three. Those who contain the elements earth and water often visit the crocodiles and alligators. These beautiful brown and green fourth-dimensional dragons help them to appreciate their surroundings and the world of nature.

Like all cold-blooded creatures, crocodiles have no emotional body. But they feel the heartbeat of the Earth in a way that most humans do not.

Despite having no emotional body they follow their instincts and when a human befriends, feeds and cares for them they may choose to respond. There is a well-documented story of a crocodile in Costa Rica who was shot in the eye by a local farmer. As a result of the trauma it was not eating. Chito befriended the 17-year-old crocodile and called him Pocho. Chito fed him chickens and other food and gave him affection until he gained the reptile's trust. Then they did shows and played together for 20 years before the crocodile died of natural causes.

Crocodiles guard their eggs fiercely and carry the babies to water when they hatch but after that the offspring are on their own. Female alligators stay with their young and will guard them for up to six months. They teach them survival skills and communicate with them with grunts. This is fourth-dimensional behaviour.

These creatures are on their ascension path to the fourth dimension.

VISUALIZATION TO CONNECT WITH CROCODILES AND ALLIGATORS

1. Find a place where you can be quiet and undisturbed.

2. Visualize yourself sitting in a sturdy boat about 10 metres from a sleeping crocodile or alligator.

3. As you tune in to the energy body of the huge reptile become aware of the extraordinary movement of light around it.

4. From its body golden and green links reach out to Neptune and from there to distant universes and planes. Vibrating light pours back down from these distant planes into the crocodile or alligator, which acts as a transformer.

5. You sense or see rich green and gold lines flow from beneath it into Hollow Earth. The light from the cosmos now streams down into the Great Pyramid in the centre of Hollow Earth to be processed.

6. At the same time knowledge and information is released from the Great Pyramid and flows into the reptile.

7. Its energy field is a pulsing wave of sacred geometric shapes, spreading in moving fingers across the land as it imparts information to the land, water, trees and any creatures it touches, including yourself.

8. Watch for a moment in awe and thank the crocodile or alligator for its service work.

9. Then open your eyes and contemplate the work these amazing creatures do.

Chapter 2

Snakes

Message from the Snakes

We bring you messages of transformation, expectation of change or even warnings. But most of you know this. The most important message we bring you is to look at your essence. Try to discover your divine blueprint. When you are in touch with who you truly are you will always act in accordance with divine will.

For thousands of years, snakes have been a source of fascination, fear, respect and even awe. They have long been recognized as messengers of metamorphosis and much more. In some cultures, they, or their skins, are considered sacred.

A snake may come to you to tell you it is time for transformation. You must now burst out of your skin and expand your life. For example, if you see a snakeskin it may be reminding you that you have to look for a new job or go on holiday or keep an eye open for an opportunity. Something new is waiting to be presented.

They come to you to warn you or tell you to look beyond the obvious. For example, I was with a friend's partner when I saw a magnificent adder. I watched it in awe. I also noted the message and stayed watchful. The friend's partner turned out to be a snake in the grass! So if you see a snake look for the reality, the true person.

Snakes are also a symbol of protection. If you call on the snake kingdom with trust and sincerity they will protect you energetically from the harm others can cause you. Snake magic has always been considered to be particularly potent.

A few days before the unicorns came to me for the first time I was sitting in my garden typing away on my laptop. I looked down to see a long smooth snake curled up beside my chair. It was absolutely beautiful. I got up quietly and moved away to call my house guest who I knew would love to see it. By the time he came downstairs the snake was gliding majestically across the lawn and disappeared into a hazel cluster. I suppose I should not have been surprised at the expansion in consciousness I received the following week. I was typing away at *The Web of Light* in exactly the same place when a white light appeared behind me. It was a unicorn and it asked me to write about unicorns in *The Web of Light* and then a book about unicorns. Those wondrous pure white illumined beings have been with me ever since and really changed my life.

All reptiles come from other universes and still carry their original divine blueprint. This is the essence that was given to them by Source when they were created. This has never been tampered with or changed and it offers them purity and power. They step down through Neptune and bring the light of their home planets with them. They can access the knowledge, wisdom and comfort of their planets of origin at any time.

Like all those who step down through Neptune, snakes carry spiritual light as well as keys and codes from Atlantis and Lemuria. As they crawl on the ground they spread this into the land for others to access.

In addition, because they are touching the earth at all times, they reach down energetically into Hollow Earth and are able to connect with the wisdom and incredible knowledge held here. They keep the history of Earth alive by bringing these records up so that people can remember them.

Some snakes are venomous, others merely bite, while others use their strength to crush their prey. This was decided at the beginning in order to try out what worked best. Earth is not just a mystery school. It is an experimental station.

Like all reptiles they sense fear in humans and react to it. If you stay totally calm and relaxed while with them, they will not harm you. In Egyptian and other times disciples went through incredibly challenging initiations. Very often the person died if they failed the test. The ability to remain calm and centred in a tank of snakes was considered to be a very high initiation test in many ancient cultures. Because there is a huge fear of snakes in the collective unconscious, this initiation also tested the student's ability to overcome the limitations of the collective unconscious.

Reptiles are not connected to a particular angel but many elementals look after them. In the case of snakes, a whole range of earth, air and water elementals take care of them. The air elementals like sylphs and fairies blow lower energies from their auras. Undines, the water elementals, flow with them in the water. Goblins help them to absorb the wisdom from Hollow Earth and spread it. Snakes do not like fire so do not connect with the salamanders of fire. However, fire dragons may help to protect their journeys!

In Japan you are allowed to feed live rodents to snakes! In Tokyo Zoo there was a rat snake called Aochan, who was refusing to eat frozen rodents. So the keepers gave him a live hamster. Unbelievably this hamster was not afraid of the snake and they became friends. The hamster often slept on top of the snake. With macabre humour, the hamster was named Gohan, which means 'Meal'.

VISUALIZATION TO CONNECT WITH THE SNAKE KINGDOM

1. Find a place where you can be quiet and undisturbed.

2. Imagine that you are in a beautiful, flower-filled, tree-lined, sun-dappled clearing.

3. There is a faint, warm breeze touching your face.

4. You are aware of a movement in the centre of the glade.

5. A magnificent snake is gliding gracefully towards you.

6. With your higher perception you can see that it is harmless and you watch its sinewy movements with awe.

7. You can tell it to stop whenever you wish to so that it feels at a safe distance, and it will obey.

8. Now you can see the trail of light it leaves behind.

9. You notice its aura radiating a soft gold and green light containing pinpricks of pure gold light.

10. This shower of lights pours over your aura and you feel it glistening and tingling over you.

11. You sense it is lighting up wisdom codes within your own aura. Relax as this happens.

12. The snake nods and imparts a telepathic message.

13. Thank the snake for coming to you.

14. Expect something new.

Chapter 3

Lizards, Salamanders, Komodo
Dragons and Chameleons

Message from the Lizard Kingdom

*We are ancient wise ones who have known and loved Earth
for aeons. You humans believe you are the masters on Earth
but that is not so. You have your own particular role to play.
Tune in to different kinds of lizards for we have much to teach
you. We accept you as you are. Please accept us as we are.*

Reptiles don't learn from their experiences for they react
according to their original divine blueprint. However, they are
teaching us many diverse lessons. One of these is understanding
and acceptance of all creatures. And each reptile brings us a
message for our growth or to guide us on our pathway.

Like snakes and crocodiles, these are all very ancient
reptiles who have stepped down through Neptune from distant
universes and are bringing with them light and knowledge
from other planes of existence. Large lizards draw down more
light than small ones. This is transferred into the Great Pyramid
within Hollow Earth, then into the crystal on top of it. It is then
beamed out through the 12 portals to various stars and planets
where it can be recorded and used.

And all these reptiles serve by bringing information up from Hollow Earth. Because they are low to the ground they take the keys and codes held within the knowledge of Hollow Earth and spread it on the surface of our planet, to keep the memory of ancient wisdom alive.

Lizards

Lizards have the same service mission as snakes, though to a lesser extent. They bring in wisdom from their planets of origin in other universes. Once incarnated they act as transformers and the information is downloaded to Hollow Earth. Here the information is stored in the Great Crystal and beamed out to the stars through the 12 portals, magnified by the crystal on top.

Lizards are nimble and quick. They love to rest and soak in the sun and yet they are always alert. If you see one, it is suggesting you ask yourself what you really want in life? Are you playing out your parents' dreams or are you in touch with your own true soul destiny? Although they are cold-blooded creatures, paradoxically they are asking you to get in touch with your heart. Decide what you want now and visualize it, then action it.

Lizards are known for dropping their tails if they are in danger. Their tail holds their life force or vitality and they are prepared to lose this rather than die. However, it will regenerate. This is a message to all of us that it is never too late. Whatever you have lost or have to let go of, you can build your life again into something bigger and better.

Salamanders

Salamanders are amphibians, not reptiles, and the main difference is that they have moist skin. With the same soul mission as snakes and lizards above, the salamander offers a slightly different message. It suggests an opportunity is about to be offered to you but you must be prepared to change in order to meet it. This is usually an internal adjustment or change in a way of thinking. If you are ready, in accordance with the Laws of the Universe, you will attract someone or a situation that will enable you to make the transformation.

It also asks you to look after your environment.

Komodo Dragons

This huge lizard is the largest in the world, growing up to three metres long. It is a species of monitor lizard and has been living in isolation for thousands of years. It is also the most aggressive. It actively attacks and devours prey many times its size, including water buffalo.

These dragons all originate from the same distant star in another universe and their blueprint includes the capacity to lead an isolated life, so that they travel widely, spreading the wisdom of their home star in their limited part of the world. The land itself here 'feels' different because these creatures bring through different, dominant and martial, vibrations from any other.

When their energy feeds down into Hollow Earth and is passed through the crystal in the Great Pyramid to the stars, it is sent to Mars. Mars contains the dominant, aggressive energy of this universe but its ascended aspect, Nigellay, holds the energy of the true divine masculine, the peaceful warrior and powerful leader. This high-frequency light is fed back in a cycle to the Komodo Dragons and will eventually raise their frequency.

Chameleons

Demonstrating the versatility of the original divine blueprint the various different-coloured varieties of chameleon catch their prey by gluing them to their long tongues. Many types of chameleon can change colour to camouflage themselves. And so they bring humans a lesson that it is possible to change and blend in. They may even offer a warning to look beyond the obvious.

VISUALIZATION TO CONNECT WITH THE LIZARD KINGDOM

1. Find a place where you can be quiet and undisturbed.

2. Close your eyes and relax into a deep centred place.

3. Imagine that you are sitting in the cool shade of a bright-green tree while the sun is burning brightly from a deep blue sky. All is peaceful. All is safe.

4. Invite the lizards to connect with you in a totally safe way.

5. Notice a lizard basking in the sun surrounded by elementals. Does it have a message for you?

6. See a chameleon nearby on the tree, blending in with the leaves, surrounded by elves. Does it have a message for you?

7. Then be aware of a salamander near you, quietly resting, surrounded by sylphs. Does it have a message for you?

8. And you hear the ground shaking a little as a big, heavy Komodo Dragon walks towards you. It is very full and sleepy as it lies down to rest. Round it there are hosts of different elementals. Does it have a message for you?

9. Allow yourself to sink deeper into relaxation as the lizards of all kinds connect with you energetically.

10. As they do so sense the connections they are making throughout the universes and with Hollow Earth.

11. Bring this light into your heart and accept them exactly as they are.

12. Thank them for coming to you and open your eyes.

Chapter 4

Tortoises

Message from the Tortoises

*We move slowly and take everything in. We feel the love
and heartbeat of Lady Gaia and yet we are not attached to
it. We spread the higher wisdom from Jupiter and Jumbay,
yet we are not attached to this either. We experience
everything just as it is. And our message to you is to
experience all that life offers without attachment. Just be.*

Tortoises are very ancient beings and they vibrate at a fifth-dimensional frequency. Like other reptiles, tortoises step into Earth through Neptune, the planet of higher spirituality, though they originate from Jumbay, the ascended aspect of Jupiter.

Jupiter is vast and has many moons. Tortoises come from a different part of Jumbay from turtles and are influenced by another moon.

They were sent to Earth with separate though similar divine missions. The turtles were to spread their wisdom from Jumbay, Atlantis and Lemuria into the waters of Earth. The tortoises' task was to spread their wisdom from Jumbay, Atlantis and Lemuria into the earth itself. Both take knowledge from Earth and Hollow Earth back to Jumbay.

Tortoises are very sensitive and build a hard shell to protect themselves physically and energetically from the world around them. This shell is also to protect the ancient wisdom they hold.

They are land-based and, being very low on the ground, draw in light and information from Hollow Earth, the seventh-dimensional chakra in the centre of our planet.

Tortoises live very long lives. Some of the very big ones live over a hundred years and accumulate knowledge and information from Hollow Earth. They feel and understand the ley-line system of Earth. They are now helping to add energy to the golden fifth-dimensional ley-line system.

During their long lives they spread huge amounts of spiritual information through their energy fields into the land, people and animals they connect with. Smaller tortoises do the same spiritual work but to a lesser capacity.

While turtles, who are water-based, connect to Lady Gaia and Hollow Earth through Archangel Joules, tortoises make their connection through Archangel Roquiel, who works deep within the Earth. Roquiel is known as an archangel but he vibrates on a twelfth-dimensional Seraphim frequency, which is truly beyond human comprehension. His colour is black, which is the yin colour of the divine feminine. And so the tortoise is able to access and bring forward extraordinarily high-frequency wisdom from Hollow Earth, with the help of this mighty angelic being.

Tortoises demonstrate to us that it is fine to move slowly through life, enjoying and appreciating every single step of the way. When necessary they practise patience, endurance, fortitude and the ability to withdraw into silent safety.

Although reptiles have no emotional body, here is a story that demonstrates that tortoises may have feelings!

In Mombasa, Kenya, there was a 100-year-old male tortoise called Mzee living in a wildlife sanctuary.

A baby hippo was separated from his parents when a tsunami wave washed him out to sea, so wildlife rangers decided to put him with Mzee. The hippo treated the tortoise as if it was his mother. He would lick the tortoise's face and be very protective of him if anyone approached. The hippo and the tortoise would bathe and sleep together.

Because hippos generally remain with their mothers for four years, the two friends stayed together for that length of time. Then the rangers introduced the young hippo to others of his kind and the tortoise returned to his solitary life.

I feel this story demonstrates devotion and detachment.

Do practise the visualization. Then notice how you feel towards tortoises.

VISUALIZATION TO CONNECT WITH TORTOISES

1. Find a place where you can be quiet and undisturbed.
2. Picture yourself in a warm and beautiful place where you feel totally happy.
3. A giant tortoise is plodding slowly towards you.
4. Look into its eyes and see the ancient wisdom accumulated in this incarnation and the even older wisdom of its soul.
5. Take a deep breath and find yourself inside the body of the giant tortoise. You have energetically become that creature.
6. Notice how you feel as you move slowly along.
7. Notice how your shell feels.

8. Be aware that a stream of light is focusing into you from Jupiter/Jumbay. Relax.

9. Sense the cells of your body acting as a transformer, sending the light on down into Hollow Earth. This information is then being beamed from the Great Pyramid into the universe. How does this feel?

10. You are bathed in rising energy from Hollow Earth. This is full of information and wisdom. You breathe it in and spread it through the land as you walk.

11. You are leaving a trail of energy wherever you go, lighting up the path you take.

12. Relax and sense what it feels to have such a beautiful soul mission.

PART V

~

THE BIRD KINGDOM

Chapter 1

Birds

Message from the Birds

It is time for you to fly. Only your consciousness limits you.
Change your thoughts. Focus on your dreams and visions,
and expand your life. This is such an important time to be on
Earth, full of opportunities for happiness and for your soul
to grow. Follow our example, spread your wings and fly.

Birds originate from Sirius or its ascended aspect Lakumay. Those who are third-dimensional belong to a soul group of about a hundred. When their soul group ascends to Lakumay they become individualized.

Birds are different from animals, fish or insects in that they have nothing to learn. They are only here on Earth to experience and to teach.

They work with and for the angels as messengers of light and show us many angelic qualities. For example, they express pure unconditional joy by singing in all weathers. They take us beyond the collective unconscious limitation of humanity by exhibiting that it is possible to fly in a physical body. They also demonstrate freedom as they soar in the sky. They literally show us it is possible to be free as a bird. And they demonstrate that you can rise above a challenge or problem.

Teaching

Most birds fly very fast and often in close proximity but their very advanced sonar ensures that they do not collide. These creatures have been the inspiration for many of our flying inventions.

No one can trap, cage or imprison a bird unless it allows it. They are with us to teach and will only let themselves be caught if there is something for humans to learn. For example, a bird may let itself be mauled by a cat to bring forward compassion or trapped in order to open someone's heart.

An eagle may let itself be caught and chained as part of an exhibit or demonstration to let people who would not otherwise do so, see for themselves how majestic and beautiful they are when they fly.

Feathers

The angels use the feathers of different birds to give people reassurance or messages that they are near. Usually they blow these feathers into the right place, often somewhere it is physically impossible for it to be. Occasionally the angels will manifest a feather but this takes energy which can often be better used for something else. If you find an unusual feather like a peacock or eagle feather, meditate on what message the bird is bringing you.

Feathers can be various colours and all have a meaning. You never find a feather by chance.

White is a pure message from the angels to say they are with you.

Black suggests it is time to listen to your inner wisdom. It may also guide you to be careful about what you are doing or saying.

Black and white are the yin yang colours, which remind you to balance your masculine and feminine energy or to bring your life into balance. Are you working too hard? Are you on too strict a diet? Are you being too nice?

Grey infers it would be helpful to ground your energy to take in the angelic light.

Blue says that the angels are bringing you healing. If it is a light blue they may be guiding you to communicate with tact and integrity.

A bright-red feather comes to you when you need to put verve and energy into something. The angels will help you.

An orange feather reminds you to open your heart and be warm and welcoming.

A pink feather calls on you to give and receive love.

A yellow feather suggests you should think things through logically.

You may live in a location where there are no birds with bright plumage. In that case if the angels want to bring you a special message a dyed feather will appear in your life!

Dawn Chorus

Every morning as the sky lightens for sunrise certain birds begin to sing. The blackbirds start, followed by the robins, wrens, thrushes, finches and hedge sparrows. There are physical reasons for this such as mating songs, catching the early worm, etc., but the spiritual reason is much simpler. These birds are entrusted to sing in the messages of the angels for that day. Each type of bird brings in a different aspect of the daily news.

These messages do not just herald good or bad weather. They remind all creatures to leave the area if there is to be an earthquake. They tell animals to shelter from storms.

They sing in the Christ Light, which is held at the ninth-dimensional frequency within Lakumay, the ascended aspect of Sirius. The Christ Light is stepped down to a vibration people can access.

They tell of cosmic changes, of best times to harvest, of the energies of the moon and stars and how they will affect the planet. In the era of Golden Atlantis people could interpret and understand the messages, which were direct guidance from the higher forces. Now we have lost this ability but a few people will start to remember again soon.

Markings

As with animals, the colours or markings on birds all have relevance.

The robin has an orange breast because orange is the colour of warmth and welcome. It does not just come and sit near you while you are digging in order to look for worms. It is also reminding you to reach out to others, to be friendly and companionable.

Like white animals, white birds carry purity in their essence and are very evolved.

Reflecting Our Group Consciousness to Us

Birds represent part of the psyche. So you would only cage a bird if an aspect of you felt trapped. In some countries, where there is a feeling of impotence in the collective consciousness, it is considered 'cool' to have a caged bird. It is a reflection of people's underlying emotions.

When hedges were removed on farms and new homes were built in suburbia, separated by fences without greenery, the homes of hedgerow birds disappeared. The little birds declined. At the same time big predatory crows, rooks and magpies started to invade towns and villages. This coincided with big businesses spreading their tentacles across the world and leaving no room for local trades and products.

It is interesting that in the 1990s around the parks of London different species of wild parakeets established themselves. They are bright, colourful, exotic, noisy and different from our local breeds, heralding waves of immigration. Parakeets also teach about communication on all levels. They were suggesting it is time for people to listen to each other, that immigrants want to be heard and accepted.

VISUALIZATION TO CONNECT WITH THE BIRDS

1. Find a place where you can be comfortable and relaxed.

2. Breathe easily until you feel yourself settling into your chair.

3. Find yourself sitting on a hillside overlooking undulating countryside.

4. You can hear birds singing everywhere round you.

5. As you relax one bird lands in front of you and hops towards you.

6. You sense it is totally friendly and wants to communicate.

7. It cocks its head and looks at you for a while. Then you sense its heart opening.

8. A golden light, the Christ Light, pours from its heart and touches yours.

9. As your heart opens you receive a message from your new friend.

10. You may sit quietly with it until it flies away.

Chapter 2

~

Fifth-dimensional Birds
from Lakumay

Message from the Fifth-dimensional Birds

*We fly or swim with enlightened eyes. Wherever we are
we look for the highest perspective. Each one of us is
unique and yet we feel the oneness of the universe. See
us with new eyes for we have much to teach you, much
more than is revealed here. Stay open to the messages
we bring to you individually and collectively from the
angelic kingdom for they can transform your life.*

These birds have ascended into the fifth-dimensional
frequency and individualized. Some are huge and some
tiny! Size is not important. Only the energy matters.

Albatrosses

These birds are huge with a vast wingspan, up to four metres
long. They spend almost all their time over water or floating
on it and this element keeps their energy fields clear. This
awesome bird is totally serene and at peace as it soars over its
territory. It can glide for hours demonstrating its total mastery
of the element air. It teaches majesty, serenity and power.

They lay only one egg at a time and both the male and female albatross care for their single chick together, showing a perfect balance of masculine and feminine energy.

These special birds spread light containing the codes of knowledge from Sirius and its ascended aspect Lakumay into the oceans. They are directed by the angels to the places where their light is most needed.

Condors

Andean condors are huge and impressive birds, one of the largest in the world that are able to fly, and are extremely heavy for their size. They have a vast three-metre wingspan. Nevertheless, they need some help so they live in windy mountains, breezy coasts or in deserts where there are strong thermal air flows. Here they demonstrate their mastery of air by gliding and swooping on the currents.

Condors are vultures. They constantly watch for carrion and it is part of their service mission to clean up their territory. There is something unassuming in being a great and gracious Master and at the same time cleaning up the leftovers of other creatures. The Andean and Californian condors have bald heads to symbolize humility and surrender to God, just as monks do.

Eagles

Eagles too are masters of air. Not only do they demonstrate how glorious it is to soar gracefully on the thermals, they make it look very simple and easy. They remind us to relax and flow with the currents of life. They also teach about enlightenment and seeing from a higher perspective.

The mighty Archangel Butyalil is teaching us the same lesson, how to flow with the universal currents at a higher level. As he does this he helps us to see our own magnificence. Look at an eagle flying high and recognize who you truly are.

Hummingbirds

Like most people, whenever I see a hummingbird I am enchanted. Their brilliant, shimmering colours reflect the radiance of the archangels. With their wings whirring so fast you can hardly see them, they have perfect balance as they draw nectar from beautiful blooms.

These tiny birds have ascended to Lakumay and carry the wisdom of the Golden Age of Lemuria in their energy fields. When you see one or even think of one or look at a picture of one, the knowledge and light of Lemuria is passed to you. They wake memories, in those people who are ready, of the love of nature, the perfect cooperation and coordination that enabled everything to flow easily in that golden time.

Owls

Owls are extraordinary ascended birds. They are universally known as wise owls because they bring wisdom from Lakumay with them. They also carry energy that helps enlighten people.

At night they teach the elementals in their area. They offer them knowledge, information and wisdom, to enable them to ascend more easily.

Each owl is in charge of an area and they clear any lower energies from their terrain. They also protect the elementals who live there.

For aeons owls have held the higher vision for the planet as it becomes fifth-dimensional. They try to impress on people what needs to be done. And this is becoming more important as we approach the new Golden Age.

When I was on sabbatical in the South of France I used to take my dog Venus for a walk to a lake. On the way we had to cross a piece of rough land and there would nearly always be a black cat on duty at the entrance. We also used to see an owl here. Cats watch, protect and clear unwanted energies from their territory just as owls do. One day they told me that they worked together to keep this area clear and protected. I was amazed and tell the full story in my e-book *Venus in France, The Spiritual Journey of a Dog on Holiday*.

The Parrot Family

All members of the parrot family – budgerigars, cockatoos, parakeets, lovebirds and macaws – have ascended into the fifth dimension and come from Lakumay. They radiate glorious colours, carrying the light and lessons of the archangels.

These advanced birds use tools. This is partly because they are using the opportunity of incarnating on Earth to develop their skills and partly to teach us that birds do have acumen.

Their greatest talent, however, is the ability to mimic words and sounds. They can copy human voices and other animals. They have acquired this ability by fine-tuning their listening skills. When you see a parrot it is reminding you to listen, not just with your ears but with your heart. Listen to feel and understand. Listen to copy. Listen to adapt.

Penguins

These delightful waddling birds are flightless, showing us that birds are special even if they cannot fly. They spend most of their time in the water, catching their food, but they live on land. The water keeps their energy fields pure and high frequency, as does the ice and snow amidst which many of them live.

They are black and white, the yin yang colours of the Earth Star chakra. In their case they have chosen to display these colours because they are deeply connected to Earth. For some creatures black and white are the colours of groundedness and total balance.

Penguins demonstrate their masculine-feminine balance in this way. The male and female birds care for their eggs and chicks together, performing different but equal tasks. In their quest to care for their chicks they show tremendous courage and devotion. They are also very protective and caring, both high-frequency qualities.

In the case of emperor penguins, the female leaves the male to look after the egg and chick. This is showing us that there are many ways to care for offspring. There is no judgement as long as it is done for the highest good.

They are connected to Archangel Sandalphon, the mighty archangel in charge of the development of the Earth Star chakras of all creatures on Earth. This fifth-dimensional chakra is black and white when it first descends as a creature becomes fifth-dimensional. As you raise your frequency it becomes grey and, finally, when you are at the upper levels of the fifth dimension, it radiates a luminous, sparkling glorious silver.

The Earth Star chakras of the penguins are beautiful silver and it is interesting to wonder if this will reflect in its plumage in the distant future. They connect to Hollow Earth and Lady Gaia through this chakra.

Puffins

This distinctive bird has a black back and white underparts. With its black head and brightly coloured bill, it is made more fascinating by its red-and-black eye-markings and bright orange legs, which suggest lightness and fun. Their masculine and feminine energies are balanced and they both care for the eggs and their pufflings. They demonstrate that it is possible to be free and joyful within a framework of responsibility.

Puffins are smaller and gentler than penguins. They too spend much of their time in the sea, where they dive for food. This keeps their energies bright and clear.

They teach us that you can be connected to the planet either through water or earth. While penguins connect to Hollow Earth through Archangel Sandalphon, the puffins make their link through the Universal Angel Joules, the archangel in charge of the oceans.

Swans

When you see a swan gliding majestically across a lake, it has regal qualities. Its white feathers signify that it is pure and the serenity with which it glides indicates a calmness within. Like any creature, if roused a swan can be powerful and fierce. However, it radiates the message in its aura that it can defend itself when challenged, so that it rarely has to do more than hiss or spread its wings. The white swans teach about beauty, grace and peace.

Black swans carry divine feminine wisdom. They also spread grace, peace, acceptance and tranquillity.

Swans teach that when you are in equilibrium and calm, all creatures honour and respect you.

VISUALIZATION TO CONNECT WITH FIFTH-DIMENSIONAL BIRDS

1. Find a place where you can be quiet and undisturbed.
2. Close your eyes and relax.
3. Imagine you are outside in beautiful countryside, with a blue sky overhead and soft warm sunshine stroking you.

4. A bird appears in your scene, carrying something for you in its beak.

5. Hold out your left hand and it drops this gift into it. It is something important for you.

6. Look at the gift and sense what the message is for you.

7. Watch the bird moving or flying away and let the lesson it is teaching everyone filter into your consciousness.

8. Mentally thank it for coming to you and if appropriate place the gift in your heart.

9. Open your eyes and start to see the birds in a new light.

Chapter 3

〜

Third-dimensional Birds

Message from the Third-dimensional Birds

We want you to understand that an eagle is not better than a sparrow. Nor is a hummingbird better than a crow. They are just vibrating on different frequencies and have unique lessons to teach you. We chose what lessons we want to bring to you and the medium through which we will present it, rather like a lecturer chooses their subject and how to teach it. You are unique and special whatever frequency you vibrate at.

All the third-dimensional birds belong to a group soul and are teaching us lessons by demonstrating them in their own lives. They come from or step down through Sirius.

Gulls

Gulls are noisy and quarrelsome. They bully smaller birds and sometimes even people. They steal food or are opportunistic in grabbing what is available. In this they are mirroring lower human behaviour. But when they rise up and fly or glide in harmony in the ethers above us they show us that it is possible to rise above the ego self. They remind us to link into our higher selves and act with the highest intentions.

Birds of Prey

This group includes hawks, falcons, buzzards, kites, harriers, ospreys, merlins and secretary birds.

Hawks have many of the attributes of eagles in that they can glide on the currents and have acute sight from above and sense the tiniest movement of prey below. They are still part of a group soul as they are not as evolved as their cousins. However, they still demonstrate that you can hold your vision and take action when the time is right.

The secretary bird of South Africa walks the savannahs of that continent but it can fly perfectly well. It was named by the Europeans who saw them and thought they looked like the male secretaries of that time with grey tailcoats and dark knee-length trousers. It demonstrates to us that beyond a very sober and stately appearance you can watch what is happening from a higher perspective and fly above it.

Hedgerow Birds

There was a time when all gardens and fields were bounded with hedges that were alive with little birds – sparrows, thrushes, cuckoos, warblers, dunnocks, nuthatches, blackbirds, tits, robins, larks, warblers, redwings, whitethroats, finches, treecreepers, wrens and chaffinches. These are songbirds that broadcast the daily messages of the angels. Their soul purpose is to keep us informed about the cosmic energies, when to plant or harvest crops, the weather, floods, earthquakes. They live near people in order to show us that there are many ways to live our domestic lives.

The cuckoo warns of the challenges of bringing up the offspring of another and suggests discernment.

The wren is quick and restless. Both male and female bring up the chicks.

Most larks are social birds who live in flocks. Some are solitary. Each shows us a different way of living life.

Migratory Birds

A surprising number of species, including swallows, swifts, martins and most geese, migrate to a different part of the world or their country to over-winter or over-summer. The above birds are reminding us of the wisdom of Lemuria. At that time, they learned to fly in patterns where they take it in turns to forge ahead for a time, then drop back and let another bird take over. They work in total harmony without leadership and demonstrate that we can do better and move faster when we work together rather than when we are solitary. They carry Lemurian healing in their energy fields and as they fly over the world they pour healing over it to nature and all creatures on Earth. They also link into the ley lines and light them up, helping to keep them clear and bright.

They never fly alone, for Archangel Bhokpi (the angel of birds) and his angels accompany them.

Ostriches, Emus, Cassowaries, Rheas and Kiwis

These are all flightless birds who are teaching us about adaptability. Because they cannot fly they had to find another way of protecting themselves. The ostrich, emu, cassowary and rhea are large birds who can run incredibly fast from danger. The kiwi, the emblem of New Zealand, is small, about the size of a hen, but it can run as fast as a human. These birds all have a huge kick and great claws so they are by no means defenceless. They demonstrate that if you cannot do something one way, you must develop another way to do it.

These birds are all sociable yet protective with each other. And they are immensely curious. They know there is much to learn.

New Zealand's giant moa is now extinct. It was hunted to extinction by humans on the physical Earth. However, as with all extinct creatures, it is well and active in its etheric body in Hollow Earth. In some future era when our outer and inner planet becomes seventh-dimensional, extinct creatures will re-emerge. Nothing is lost forever.

What I love about these flightless birds is their unique contract with Lady Gaia. Because they agreed to lose their ability to fly in order to demonstrate there is another way to live your life, they receive extra support from the angels and elementals. Wherever you see one of these birds running away from harm there is a whole host of angels and elementals with them. Fairies particularly fly with them and guide them.

Peacocks and Birds of Paradise

I love peacocks. I remember the thrill of looking across the Ganges at sunset. Every hundred yards or so single peacocks, trailing their gorgeous tails, emerged from the trees to go down for a drink. I was with my daughter and we then travelled down to Agra where she bought me a marble plate inlaid with a peacock which I still have on the wall in my sitting room.

The peacock is flamboyant, beautiful and egotistical. All eyes turn to look at him when he spreads his glorious fan tail. His cry is loud, shrill and demands attention. However, there is a higher purpose for this. While everyone is looking at the male his smaller, dull-brown female can safely bring up their chicks.

So the peacock and peahen demonstrate that sexes can be totally different yet work together for the highest good. They also teach us to look beyond the outward appearance to see what is really happening.

The male bird of paradise, with its brightly coloured extravagant plumage, is a wondrous sight to behold. As with the peacock, the hen bird of paradise is dull in comparison. But she watches intently as the male parades, deciding who would be the best provider of genetic material. She is teaching the art of careful and precise decision-making. In this case the lesson is: Be aware of and enjoy the show but be clear about what you are looking for.

Songbirds

This group includes finches, larks, warblers, tits, robins, starlings, sparrows, treecreepers, wrens, dippers, lyrebirds, babblers, siskins, bramblings, mockingbirds, buntings, nightingales, weavers and cardinals, and most of them sing beautifully.

Have you ever sat in your garden or been out for a walk when you have seen a little bird singing its heart out to you? If so pause for a moment and listen for it is bringing you a message. It is singing to you of your divine magnificence.

In rain, snow or sunshine songbirds sing from their hearts. The angels are pouring their communications through them. They are mating songs but they are also individual messages. Birds multi-communicate! In the golden era of Atlantis people could understand these downloads but now we have lost the ability. Nevertheless, at an unconscious level we can still tune in to the information we are being given.

And even though a bird may sing the same song over and over again to our ears, each time it does so it carries a different message.

The lyrebird has a beautiful song, but can also mimic almost anything; from other bird calls to car alarms. I watched a video clip on the Internet where a magnificent lyrebird was imitating everything from clicking camera shutters to chainsaws. Like parrots they are really tuned in to the art of listening.

Some species of weaver birds are master builders, creating incredibly intricate and beautiful nests with knowledge they have brought with them from Sirius. Some are spectacular. Others are untidy.

The most striking of the songbirds is the male northern cardinal, a bright, glorious red, shining out and singing sweetly in winter snow or summer sun.

All songbirds offer inspiration.

Chickens

Chickens originally arrived with the service animals at the start of the Golden Age of Atlantis. They came specifically to give humans their feathers and eggs, which the people of that time accepted with grace and gratitude.

Because their service work is to offer their eggs, many of them cluck contentedly when they lay one. They are demonstrating that they are happy to give.

They come from a distant asteroid in the tenth-dimensional universe of Shekinah and step their frequency down through Sirius. These little creatures carry love and joy beyond our comprehension in their energy fields.

They are also here to teach humans that service is an important part of our ascension path.

Crows, Rooks, Magpies, Drongos and Ravens

These birds are all tricksters, magicians and agents of transition. They take messages from Archangel Azriel, the angel of birth and death, to animals and humans. If an animal is ready to give birth one of these birds will appear to her to remind her to prepare for the new arrival.

In addition, one of these birds will come to you if it is time for you to expect change or to raise your vibration. As such they are messengers of enlightenment, telling you to see things from a higher perspective and to raise your frequency towards your challenges.

In former times the people recognized that ill fortune sometimes befell people when a single member of the crow family appeared. In fact, they are reminding you to look at higher possibilities and make changes. So if you see a single one of these birds watch your thoughts and intentions.

While their soul mission is to help people towards enlightenment, their service mission is to eat carrion, to keep everything clean and make sure everything is used.

These birds are highly intelligent. Black drongos can imitate other birds. They can use the warning calls of other birds or even meerkats to trick them into abandoning their food so that the drongos can eat it. They constantly change tactics.

Pigeons, Doves, Partridge, Plovers, Grouse and Pheasants

These birds work with the Angels of Peace and Love. The soul work of pigeons is similar to that of ducks. People throw bread or seeds to them, unaware that the birds are bringing them messages of love and harmony. Not surprisingly in these times pigeons are flocking in towns, reminding us of the need for peace.

The soul work of partridges, plovers, grouse and pheasants is to spread the message of love and peace in the countryside.

Their service work is to peck the ground, to prepare it for seeds to grow.

Toucans

Everyone knows the toucans because of their huge colourful beak. They live in small flocks, and their bright plumage provides them with camouflage in the tropical rainforests of Central America, South America and the Caribbean.

They have very small wings, so they tend to hop around the trees in the rainforest. Their large bill is very light and helps them to keep cool in the hot climate. Arteries in their bill expand when they get hot and release heat. They have one of the best heat-regulating systems in the bird and animal kingdoms. Their service mission is to demonstrate to humans in hot countries that there are many ways of regulating their temperature. It is also about using the gifts you have for the highest good and always being ready to adapt.

Vultures

While the condor is fifth-dimensional, most vultures are not. They are scavengers, and they demonstrate to us how important it is to keep our environment clear and clean. Nature is economical. Everything has a purpose and nothing ever needs to be wasted.

VISUALIZATION TO LEARN FROM THE BIRDS

1. Find a place where you can be quiet and undisturbed.
2. Close your eyes and allow yourself to relax.
3. Think of a bird and call it to you or you can just allow any bird to appear in your mind's eye.
4. Mentally tell the bird that you are willing to learn from it and ask for a communication or demonstration.

5. The bird may sing to you, in which case relax and let the message flow into your heart.

6. If the bird shows you a picture, ask yourself what the message is.

7. The bird may communicate with you telepathically, so stay open to learn.

8. Thank the bird and look out for one of this type in your life or in a book or on television.

9. If you see one know it is confirming that it is bringing you an important message.

Alternatively, you can go out into your garden, a park or the countryside and watch to see what birds are showing themselves to you.

Chapter 4
~

Water Birds

Message from the Water Birds

Water carries the unifying love force of the world and
we live in it and pass it on to you. Love wants you to be
happy and at peace. It wants your visions and dreams
to manifest for your highest good. When you see one of
us we remind you to ignore the outer drama. Instead be
aware that love is the essence of every person and animal.
Focus on your heart's desire so that you draw it into your
life. Let it enrich your days and spread joy into the world.

Water carries the love energy of the universe and as
such it is the glue that holds the cosmos and all of us
together. Water birds are kept clear and pure by this energy
and they also carry and spread love in their auras. They all have
special messages for us and lessons to teach us.

The birds in this section are all third-dimensional and come
from Sirius.

Ducks, Moorhens and Coots

These birds all work with the Angels of Peace. I love to think
of children taking bread to feed the ducks, unaware that the

birds are bringing them messages to stay calm, peaceful and in harmony. Sometimes the birds are connecting the child directly to the Angels of Peace. No wonder children love to feed the ducks.

Ducks, moorhen and coots pull on the water weed to loosen the roots and mud so that new growth can establish itself.

As the new Golden Age approaches and the world comes into more harmony, we will recognize these birds for who they really are.

Kingfishers, Storks, Herons and Cranes

These birds keep their energy clear by living near water. They demonstrate to us patience and the power of holding a positive vision or intention. Their goal is a fish and by their focused intent, they attract a fish to them. The instant their goal is in sight they take action and catch it.

A kingfisher, like a rainbow or ladybird, causes most people to gasp with delight when they see it and this opens doors of opportunity in the universe. So if you see one it asks you to keep your thoughts and intentions pure.

Pelicans

These interesting birds originally appeared in the time of Mu, the age of the dinosaurs. Pelicans look like dinosaurs, carrying as they do the keys and codes of that civilization. You cannot watch a pelican without unconsciously thinking of Mu, a time when the beings loved Earth and nature. You then automatically tune in to the collective memory of that time. They also remind us that our planet has been operating for aeons. Earth is ancient and will continue regardless of what we humans do.

Wading Birds

Flamingos, oystercatchers, ibises, avocets, bitterns and many shoreline birds spend their time in water, which keeps them clear and in the cosmic energy of love. While they have not mastered this element, they work in harmony with it. When you see one it reminds you subliminally that water is healing and purifying.

These birds see through the outer show into the truth, into the purity. They bring us a message to forget the drama, do what is right, keep things simple and go with the flow.
The pink flamingos teach: go with the flow with love.

VISUALIZATION TO CONNECT WITH THE WATER BIRDS

1. Find a place where you can be quiet and undisturbed.
2. Give yourself time to relax and unwind.
3. Find yourself by a beautiful stretch of water and breathe in the energy of your inner scene.
4. Think of your vision, something you really want to create in your life.
5. Become aware of a long-legged bird standing in the water, staring intently down into the pure clear liquid.
6. As you do so strengthen your focus on your vision. The collective energy of this bird is with you.
7. Watch the bird as it takes action and catches a fish.
8. Decide what action you are going to take.
9. Suddenly, in a flash of iridescent turquoise, a kingfisher passes you with a fish in its beak.
10. Be aware of a rainbow forming in the sky and know that a doorway is opening for you.
11. Imagine yourself walking through the doorway into your manifest vision.
12. Thank the bird energy that is still helping you.

PART VI

THE INSECT
KINGDOM

I use the generic term insects for all those creatures under the care of Archangel Preminilek.

Bees, beetles and invertebrates with six legs, a head, thorax and abdomen are insects.

Scorpions, ticks and spiders are arachnids.

Slugs and snails are molluscs.

Centipedes and millipedes are myriapods.

Earthworms are annelids, but there is a diverse range of worms.

Chapter 1

Fourth- and Fifth-dimensional Insects

Message from the Fourth- and Fifth-dimensional Insects

We are honoured to bring you healing, love, light, messages and wisdom from our home planets. We have so much more to offer you than Diana has been able to share. This is the tip of the iceberg.

We ask you to be open to our messages and knowledge for this will expand your consciousness and your joy. When you in turn honour and respect us it adds to your light and to that of the insect kingdom for we are all part of the oneness.

There would not be a world without insects for they play a vital role in keeping our ecosystems healthy. They break down organic matter and enrich our soil. They even provide food for larger animals in the food chain. Bees and other insects are essential to our survival because they pollinate plants including many of our food crops.

Some insects, like the dragonflies, demonstrate advanced sacred geometry and aerial manoeuvres. Others spread healing. All have a sacred mission on Earth and intend to take their learnings back to their planet of origin.

There are millions of different kinds of insects, all belonging to group souls, and this is more than all the other animal and plant species combined.

Many insects are third-dimensional. A few vibrate in the fourth and fifth dimensions. Archangel Preminilek, assisted by various elementals, looks after them all, coordinates their service work and helps them ascend to a higher frequency.

Insects are on a very different wavelength to humans. It is more difficult for us to tune in to their frequency band though it is easier to communicate with those insects who radiate a higher vibration.

I know many people, including myself, who ask the ants who are in the house and are highly evolved, to move to a more appropriate location. I remember my surprise when I first did this many years ago and the ants actually trailed off to the place where I had offered them a safe refuge (in the garden).

Fifth-dimensional insects

Ants

These valiant little creatures have stepped down from Lakumay, the ascended aspect of Sirius, bringing their knowledge of sacred geometry with them. They operate on a very high-frequency band and with pure intention. Their higher purpose or soul mission is to learn and teach about sacred geometry. They demonstrate its principles when they build their nests.

When anything is constructed according to sacred geometry, whether it is a cathedral, a house or a nest, the formations vibrate at such a high frequency that they produce magical harmonies. Every object in this world radiates out a vibration and a note. If you have crafts that are handmade with love in your home they emit beautiful harmonics, raising the frequency of your rooms. Mass-produced artefacts send out the energies of the workshops in which they are made. Anything made according to sacred geometry creates pure light in the etheric and vibrates with angelic harmonies.

Ants' nests, lovingly constructed with sacred geometry, form angelic magnets, drawing in the angels to sing over their homes. And all kinds of elementals are attracted to their nests so that they can soak in the angelic light that surrounds them.

Ants also teach about structured family life, and how to live collectively in a cooperative way for the highest good of all. The ant has two stomachs. One for himself, the other for food to share.

Ants can move very quickly. If we humans could move as fast for our size as an ant, we could run as fast as a racehorse. They can also lift 20 times their own body weight. They are little spiritual warriors. Their service work is to build tunnels that aerate the soil, to decompose organic waste and help keep the environment clean.

Bees

Without bees we could not survive on our planet because they are the main pollinating agents of Earth. They offer this huge service to us as part of their fifth-dimensional service mission.

Bees come from the Pleiades. I read that the honeybees travel an average of 43,000 miles to collect enough nectar to make a pound of honey! And throughout this journey they spread blue Pleiadean heart healing. Honey itself has many healing properties.

Part of the work of the pixies is to ensure that the bees pollinate as many flowers as they can.

My childhood memories include sitting in sunlit wildflower meadows, always accompanied by the buzz of bumble bees who were probably pouring their heart healing onto me. So much happens that we are not aware of.

The hives of the bees are built on sacred geometrical principles, so where there is a hive, there are angels singing. Here fairies and many other elementals also gather to bathe in the angelic vibrations for this helps their evolution.

Their soul mission is to teach about sacred geometry and to spread Pleiadean heart healing.

Butterflies and Moths

Everyone loves butterflies, who originate from Orion, as do moths. They both come from the planet of wisdom and carry this light in their energy fields. This is the ability to know how to use information or to do something for the highest good of all.

These special fifth-dimensional insects are emissaries of the angels. Whenever you see one fluttering in the gardens or meadows they are bringing you a message. It may be a general one to remind you that you are a beloved child of the universe. It may be prompting you to look at the marvels of the world around you or to open your eyes to see something particular. It may be helping you to keep up your spirits or whispering to you of joy and bliss.

Sometimes it is bringing a special message from a loved one. When a friend of mine died young in an accident, a butterfly flew through the window onto the table laid for tea at the funeral. Her fiancé immediately knew it was coming to tell him she was happy in spirit and all was in divine right order.

The auras of butterflies contain energies that can help us to connect to the Illumined angels.

Their service work is to pollinate. They may not be as efficient as bees but they glide and flutter from flower to flower, filling us with delight as we watch them. To bring joy and delight is part of their soul mission.

Butterflies go through the most extraordinary metamorphosis to transform from egg to caterpillar to cocoon and finally to emerge as glorious winged creatures. They are demonstrating to us that transformation is possible. Monarch caterpillars shed their skin four times before they become a chrysalis. They grow to over 2,700 times their original size. This is a message that huge spiritual growth is possible in our lifetimes.

And individual kinds of butterfly develop local survival mechanisms. For example, some types of night butterflies have ears on their wings so they can avoid bats!

Many insects are teaching us lessons of adaptability.

Children's illustrations often show fairies playing with or riding on butterflies. Those painters were seeing through the veils for fairies and butterflies have a natural connection. Fairies direct butterflies and are always there to help them when they emerge from their cocoons and first spread their wings.

I remember once sitting on a hillside on a hot sunny day quietly tuning in to what was going on around me. I became aware of a caterpillar that crawled into the middle of the dusty path and lay there, totally vulnerable to birds or being trampled on. Two brownies, little air elementals, were trying to persuade it to move back into the shelter of a bush. It listened for a while and did gradually move to safety. There was a sense of relief for a few moments but then it defiantly crawled back into its former exposed position. The brownies just sat patiently beside it and were still there when I moved away.

Ladybirds

Ladybirds are not just a symbol of good luck. These pretty little beetles actually do bring happiness and good fortune to you. If you see one and gasp with pleasure, your energy shift at that moment opens doors of joy and blessings for you from the universe.

Originating from Orion, the service mission of these delightful fifth-dimensional beings is to consume aphids that are destroying our crops.

At a soul level they are working with the elemental kingdom to help plants. The air elementals – the fairies and sylphs – blow away any lower energies that gather round flora and fauna, and the ladybirds help this process.

They also communicate with other insects. As fifth-dimensional beings they have a higher perspective on what is happening and they try to persuade other insects who are harming plants to move elsewhere.

Ladybirds spread angelic qualities wherever they go, which people and animals unconsciously sense. They spread love, peace, wisdom, joy, harmony and cooperation.

Fourth-dimensional insects

When humans, animals and insects are self-interested they are third-dimensional. As their hearts open and they become concerned about the welfare of others and the world around them, they become fourth-dimensional.

Whatever their level of spiritual growth on Earth, each individual or group soul has received an invitation from Lady Gaia to come here and each has something to offer in return.

Dragonflies

These iridescent creatures are the most beautiful and the most interesting of insects. Like ants they step down from Sirius and have a great deal to teach us. They are fourth-dimensional because they are joyfully serving us by demonstrating advanced technology to us. They are constantly reminding us of the incredible technology of Atlantis by exhibiting what humans could accomplish at that time.

When they are hunting they calculate the distance of their prey, the direction it is moving in and the speed it is flying. In a fraction of a second they calculate the angle of its approach.

Their eyes are extraordinary. Many insects have multifaceted eyes that enable them to have a panoramic view of their surroundings. Each facet creates its own image. The dragonflies' eyes can compile 3,000 images into one picture, so they can see in all directions. They can use their advanced eye structure to lock onto their prey like a homing device. They can also manoeuvre their four wings independently of each other. This is how they hover, moving forwards, backwards and sideways, then in an instant darting off in another direction or even flying upside down. And these tiny insects can travel up to 50 miles an hour! They are regarded as the magicians of the insect world.

Scorpions

Scorpions are much feared because of their venom. When I lived in the Caribbean we had a kitten who was playing on the verandah. I could see it was pawing something so tiny and pale that it was almost invisible. She howled and jumped around at the same instant I realized it was a baby scorpion. It really hurt her so I am glad it was such a baby.

But scorpions evolved to the fourth dimension because they care for their young until they are ready to survive independently. The little ones scuttle onto the mother's back for protection.

Worms

Worms originate from Neptune, the planet of higher spirituality. They evolved into the fourth dimension because they collectively decided as an act of service to aerate the soil. They increase the amount of air and water within the earth and they break down organic matter, such as leaves and grass, in a way that plants can use it. Furthermore, they never eat living plant tissue or harm plants in any way.

I think of earthworms as very useful small creatures that I welcome in the soil. Then I saw pictures of the giant Gippsland earthworm in Australia which averages a metre in length but can be as long as three metres! I'd only need one to aerate all the soil in my garden.

Visualization to Connect with Fifth-dimensional Insects

1. Find a place where you can be quiet and undisturbed.

2. Breathe gently and invite Archangel Preminilek, the angel of insects, to be with you.

3. You may have a sense of his yellow-green light around you.

4. Be aware of an ants' nest in front of you, busy with little workers. Then tune in to the awesome angel light and sonics above it. Let this bring you into harmony.

5. Invite a bee to place a blue Pleiadean healing rose in your aura.

6. Watch a beautiful butterfly flutter in front of you and sense the message it is bringing you.

7. Let a ladybird land on or near you. Feel a surge of delight and sense a golden door in the universe open for you.

8. If you wish to, thank the fourth-dimensional insects, the dragonflies, the scorpions and the worms for all they offer our planet.

9. Know that your connection today has added to your light and to that in the insect kingdom.

10. Thank Archangel Preminilek and the insects and open your eyes.

Chapter 2

~

Third-dimensional Insects

Message from the Third-dimensional Insects

*We are here on this beautiful planet to learn and sometimes
to demonstrate what we have already learned.*

*We wish to coexist in peace and harmony with you.
Our desire is to do our service work for this enables
Earth to sustain life. Without us you would not be
here. Please acknowledge us, give us space and let
us be. We honour you and ask you to respect us.*

All the third-dimensional insects originate from Neptune
with the exception of spiders, who come from a distant
universe and step down through Sirius.

Beetles

The service mission of all beetles is to break down old, unwanted
material so that it can be recycled for a higher purpose. Their
soul purpose is to bring in light and to take knowledge back
to Neptune.

Each type of beetle is extraordinary and brings in its
own individual gift. For example, Hercules beetles can lift

850 times their own weight. That's equivalent to a human lifting 10 elephants! Currently the collective unconscious holds a belief that we can only lift a certain percentage of our body weight. These beetles are demonstrating that the sky is the limit.

Centipedes and Millipedes

Centipedes and millipedes do not have a proliferation of legs by chance! Their soul purpose is to learn and teach about coordination. They are demonstrating that it is possible for many aspects to work together in harmony.

Centipedes are also demonstrating regeneration for they can grow more legs. This is currently impossible for humans because we are limited by our collective consciousness belief. These creatures are showing us that it is possible!

Millipedes start with only a few legs but continue to grow more each time they moult. They also serve by helping to decompose organic matter in the earth.

Cockroaches

These universally disliked insects are the rats of the insect world. They have come in with an important service mission. They break down foul waste to keep nutrients moving round the ecosystem. This was fine and even gratefully accepted when humans were more fastidious and created only a little foul waste. Nowadays there are so many people on Earth that we have created a huge complex of sewerage systems and cockroaches have to proliferate and work hard to do their task. They not only work with physical dirt, they also help to clear the etheric energy around it.

They also break up the waste of other animals, including bats, and clear the low psychic energy round it.

Because so many creatures wish to be on Earth at this special time of spiritual opportunity, the cockroaches are finding their mission to be overwhelming. Esaks and kyhils are also assisting in this clearing process.

Flies

The soul purpose of these winged insects is to remind us about the importance of hygiene and cleanliness. In the golden era of Atlantis there were no flies but as the frequency of the people declined they arrived from all over the world.

Their service work at the maggot stage is to break down decaying material and help to create topsoil. They digest dead trees, animals and animal waste. As adult flies they offer themselves as food for insect-eating animals.

Fleas

Like many insects the service work of fleas is to break down organic matter to enrich the soil. Flea larvae emerge from the eggs to feed on any available organic material such as dead insects, faeces and vegetable matter. The larvae and adult flea provide food for many birds and other creatures.

Their soul purpose is to remind us of the importance of cleanliness.

Midges

These tiny bloodsucking flies have the same service mission and soul purpose as flies. They aid in the decomposition process and offer themselves as food to fish, other insects and birds. And like all creatures, they have something to demonstrate. For example, some midges beat their wings faster than any other creature and one type reaches 1,000 beats a second – awesome.

Mosquitoes

During the golden era of Atlantis the water was kept pure, clear and running, so there was no place for or need for mosquitoes. These insects poured into Atlantis as the energy started to decline to remind people to continue to keep water pure and moving.

Their soul purpose is still to remind us of this.

Slugs and Snails

Slugs and snails are molluscs who both have the same service work and soul mission. The snail carries a shell and it has to produce calcium to build and maintain it, so there are fewer of them than slugs. At a spiritual level the difference in their divine blueprint is because experiments were taking place to see how variations to the basic slug would manage on Earth.

Apparently a snail can sleep for three years without waking up. This would suggest that they go into an altered state where they connect with and are nourished by the higher light.

I know I have shared this story before but it really impressed me. When I was first asking about slugs and snails my guide Kumeka told me that they originally incarnated to eat up all the dead leaves under trees and bushes. They served happily in this way for aeons until humans started planting juicy lettuces and other delicacies that are so much tastier than withered old leaves. Kumeka said that they knew they shouldn't be eating lettuces, in the same way that I know I shouldn't be eating chocolate, but it is irresistible to them! This story really softened my heart towards all the slugs and snails in my garden. How can I be cross with them for what I do myself?

Ticks

These parasitic creatures have been on Earth for millions of years. Apparently they were the bane of dinosaurs! Their service work is to host many micro-parasites, viruses and bacteria and to offer themselves as food for reptiles, fish and birds.

However, their soul purpose is to remind us that we live in an interdependent world. When they are drawn to the blood of deer they pass it to another animal and within the blood is the lesson the deer is teaching, trust. When they bite a giraffe, they pass its energy to other animals with the wisdom of Orion.

Crickets, Grasshoppers and Locusts

These insects are all very similar and their service work is simple. They eat vast amounts of food. For example, a locust can eat its own weight in food in a day while a person takes about six months to do so. This means they produce enormous amounts of waste to fertilize the ground. They also offer themselves as food to nurture and sustain birds, animals and people.

Crickets sing by rubbing their wings together while grasshoppers rub their hind legs against their wings. Their song when slowed down sounds like a choir of heavenly music and can heal. This music holds the keys and codes of higher love from the ascended constellation of Andromeda. It also contains a message for us to slow down. This is their soul offering.

Crickets, grasshoppers and locusts can jump and fly. They jump by catapulting themselves into the air. If we could jump as far as they can we could leap the length of a football pitch with ease. They are demonstrating to us what is possible and suggest we expand our level of possibilities.

Spiders

Spiders come from a distant third-dimensional universe where there is no gravity. They are on a very different wavelength from ours and this is why they feel so alien to us. It is also why so many people dislike them or are frightened of them.

They step down through Sirius. Here they learn about sacred geometry, which they practise on Earth. Then they take all the knowledge back home with them.

They are not just here to learn. They demonstrate sacred geometry to us in their webs and teach us that it has a useful function.

They also teach us to move beyond our limitations. The collective consciousness of Earth believes in gravity. We expect everything to be magnetically drawn back to Earth and therefore it is.

Because spiders come from a plane of existence without gravity they do not have the effects of gravity programmed into their minds. They spin their webs against the pull of gravity by holding the vision of their desired outcome. The power of their collective mind is stronger than gravity. Therefore, they succeed.

The soul mission of spiders is to teach us to hold a vision with focus and determination so that we overcome the restrictions of our collective beliefs. This is a huge message and vitally important for us to understand as we move towards the expansion of the new Golden Age.

Spiders are also learning and teaching about patience, focus and determination. They are also adaptable. I loved reading about a type of spider who twangs the threads of his web like a harp to make music to attract a mate.

As with all sacred geometric structures the angels sing sonics over the webs of spiders. When I walk in the early morning and see diamond dewdrops on webs lit up by the rising run I believe in pure magic.

Indeed, one of the magic gifts spiders give to the world is their silk, which weight for weight is stronger than steel, is lightweight, ductile and can flex or stretch. All things are provided in nature and the spiders are demonstrating to us that it is possible to create such a product when we are ready.

They offer us much but their service work is to control insect populations and keep them at a reasonable level.

Wasps

The soul work of these valiant but scary little creatures is to teach us the benefits of sacred geometry by building their nests according to the methods they learned in Sirius. The angels sing over the nests creating sonics so there are always elementals around wasps' nests.

And their service mission is to pollinate, scavenge and devour insects and parasites to keep the ecological balance in harmony.

Wasps will give their lives to save their fellow wasps so they also teach about sacrifice for the greater good of the community as a whole.

VISUALIZATION TO THANK THIRD-DIMENSIONAL INSECTS

1. Find a place where you can be quiet and undisturbed.

2. Set your intention of understanding and thanking the insect kingdom.

3. You are sitting on a soft, smooth warm boulder overlooking the countryside.

4. Open your heart to the world of insects.

5. Thank the beetles for breaking down old, unwanted material so that it can be recycled for a higher purpose.

6. Thank the centipedes and millipedes for demonstrating the beauty of coordination and the possibility of regeneration.

7. Thank the cockroaches for breaking down foul waste to keep nutrients moving round the ecosystem.

8. Thank the fleas for reminding us about the importance of cleanliness.

9. Thank the flies for reminding us about the importance of good hygiene.

10. Thank the mosquitoes for reminding us to keep water clean and moving.

11. Thank the slugs and snails for eating up the dry old leaves.

12. Thank the ticks for teaching us we live in an interdependent world and for passing on the wisdom of other creatures.

13. Thank the crickets, grasshoppers and locusts for fertilizing the land and for teaching us to expand our level of possibilities.

14. Thank the spiders for demonstrating sacred geometry and teaching us the power of focusing on our vision.

15. Thank the wasps for teaching about sacred geometry, and for the work they do pollinating, scavenging and devouring insects.

16. Ask that humans and insects may live in divine harmony.

PART VII

~

THE TREE KINGDOM

Chapter 1

Trees

Message from the Trees

*We come from the heart of God with nothing to learn
and much to offer. We were seeded on Earth for the
benefit of the human, animal, bird and insect kingdom
and to nurture the planet itself, physically, emotionally
and spiritually. We radiate love and healing to you.*

Physical nurturing

Trees offer wood to build shelters, boats and anything else we
may need to construct. They provide shade from the sun and
protection from the elements.

They house animals, birds and insects.

They provide food.

Emotional nurturing

Every variety of tree carries a quality that it radiates in its auric
field to help those that seek it.

Trees and plants react to the lower thoughts of humans
and respond positively to their loving thoughts.

Trees give healing.

Spiritual nurturing

These wise sentient beings keep records of local history.

Forests are keepers of ancient wisdom. They use it to help the energy of the country in which they grow.

Large forests bring light, containing wisdom and knowledge, down from the stars and higher beings of the universes to store or to pass into Hollow Earth.

Acer, Maple, Sycamore and Plane

These trees remind you of your own inner beauty. They are very sensitive to the energies around them. They know how you feel. They take in the vulnerable feelings of humanity, then help people feel safer. They also empathize with us with gentle understanding and this allows us to strengthen ourselves. When you sit with one of these trees you start to feel better.

Ash

Ash trees hold divine feminine wisdom and impart the qualities to humans and animals.

They often choose to grow along ley lines so that they can use the divine feminine to soften the flow of energy along them. This brings a gentle and balanced energy into areas where they grow.

Their black buds symbolize that they are holding the new growth within the yin cocoon during the formation of the leaves.

If you stand under an ash tree or meditate on one during full moon you will receive an extra boost of energy. It also assists magic.

The mountain ash or rowan is very protective. Ask for protection and it will be provided.

Baobab

The baobab trees are recognizable by their distinctive swollen trunks that can hold up to 120,000 litres of water – a godsend in the arid areas in which they grow. Mature trees are often hollow and offer shelter. Apparently one baobab tree in South Africa, known as 'Big Baobab', has a circumference of 47 metres and even has a bar that can hold up to 60 people in its hollow trunk.

This is a life-giving tree, and when you sit in its protection you receive the message that you are looked after and your needs will be met. It helps to raise the frequency of people's base chakras.

This tree is found in Africa, Australia and Madagascar. It has various names:

- The Tree of Life because every part of it can be used by humans and animals.

- The Bottle Tree because it really does look like a bottle.

- The Monkey Bread Tree because its large pods are known as monkey bread and are a favourite fruit of the monkeys that live in the area. These pods are rich in vitamin C.

- The Upside-down Tree. Because the tree is leafless most of the year its bare branches look like roots sticking up into the air.

This is such an unusual-looking tree that there are legends about how it received its name.

One story tells us that when God made the world he gave each animal a tree. He gave the baobab to the foolish hyena who planted it upside down!

One African tale is that the baobab tree did not like the way it looked so it nagged God all the time for making it unattractive.

One day, God had had enough. He pulled it from the ground and turned it over, replanting it upside down so that its mouth was in the soil and it could not nag any more.

Beech

These remarkable sturdy trees really do offer grace. They help humans to find forgiveness in their hearts by attuning them to the wisdom of their past soul journey. This softens the consciousness and helps people to see things differently. When people walk through beech woods they often feel soothed and calm but do not realize that the energy reaching out to them is materially shifting their perception and feelings. The energy is raising the vibrations and enabling humans to rise above the hurt and pain.

Chestnut

The horse chestnut tree radiates an energetic quality of playfulness. It is not by chance that children, and many adults, play with conkers and have an enormous amount of fun with them. When my children were small I would automatically shuffle round in the fallen leaves to see if there were any big brown chestnuts hiding there and feel a sense of delight if I found one. It reminded me of my own childhood. This tree may be strong and sturdy but it encourages light-heartedness and innocence.

For centuries children played with the fruits of the horse chestnut but in recent years they have demanded more sophistication or technology in their play activities. Because humans and trees are so symbiotically connected, this lack of response from children has weakened the chestnut trees and allowed them to be attacked by the horse chestnut leaf-miner, a small moth whose caterpillars feed inside the leaves, leaving disfiguring blotches.

A proliferation of horse chestnuts signifies abundance and this tree sends out energy that expands you to accept abundance.

Sweet chestnut trees also hold the quality of abundance consciousness. If you want to shift your fortunes and attract a cornucopia of delight, spend time with this tree.

Both the chestnut trees will bring you hope and happiness and enable you to raise your expectations.

Conifers – Pine, Spruce and Fir

Both fir and pine trees raise your frequency and enable you to heal and regenerate. There is nothing like walking in a fir or pine forest to lift your spirits and help you feel good. They literally heal the mind and the body. These trees help people to rise to the fifth dimension.

It is not by chance that so many spas and health resorts are built in fir or pine forests, for the trees bring you back into balance and health.

In huge forests the trees store much ancient wisdom as well as the spiritual technology of the future brought by beings from other star systems. They are holding it until we are ready to access it.

Sequoias are conifers, the giants of the tree kingdom. They bring a message to remind us of the vastness of the universe and at the same time they ask us to remember who we can truly be – spiritual giants.

Yew trees symbolize transformation and rebirth. They were planted in graveyards because they are also very protective of spirits who linger there and part of their divine task is to offer them energy to help them go to the light.

Elm

When I was a child these trees grew everywhere in the UK and we were always warned not to play under them because boughs could fall off suddenly. They were known as 'widow makers'.

They are very sensitive to energies. Trees need spiritual and psychic energy and they draw this from the ley lines. Dutch elm disease has recently decimated these trees. It occurred because the ley lines were blocked when the Channel Tunnel was built. The elm trees coped with the back-up of energy in the ley lines caused by the building of the Dartford Tunnel but when the nearby Channel Tunnel was constructed soon afterwards it was too much. Those elms nearest the ley lines were affected first. Then it spread.

Dutch elm disease first killed the elm trees in the 16th century. Huge numbers of people died of the plague and where their bodies were buried on the ley lines, the trees were badly affected energetically.

We can all help the elm trees by calling in the higher light and spreading it along the ley lines. Then they can flourish once more.

These trees help you to be quick. They enable you to stand in your power but in a balanced way.

Fruit Trees

Cherry, Apple, Pear, Plum and Others

These pretty blossoming trees bring love, joy and purity. Who hasn't gasped when they have seen an avenue of pink flowering cherry or an orchard of apple trees in bloom? They lift your heart. They also bring abundance and trigger gratitude within us. And, in turn, our gratitude draws more abundance from the universe.

Olive

This tree not only holds the knowledge of its location but a great deal of wisdom. It reminds you of the long history of the Earth, and when you sit under it, it helps you connect into Hollow Earth. It also reminds you that all your needs will be met.

Hawthorn

These may not be the prettiest of trees. They are prickly and often scruffy but I love them. They are valiant protectors! If they grow round your home, they will protect you and your house. Where they grow in hedgerows they protect the animals and the space they surround. When you attune to these trees you will feel their love and also their strength and valour.

Holly

When someone is horrid or nasty they feel bad inside and they project their hurt feelings onto others. The prickly holly brings the message that we should not judge someone by their outer appearance. Look beyond that and see their hurting inner. So when you see a holly tree remember this and it can heal your feelings and cause you to behave gently to certain people.

And in the winter the red berries of the holly nurture and provide for birds. We also bring them in to decorate our home in a festive way so when we do look beyond the outer at a person's divine self we receive a reward.

Mahogany

This huge tropical tree stands in its magnificence and power, carrying the qualities of strength, dependability, reliability and trust. When people first connect with the mahogany tree they often feel a sense of their own insignificance but the tree takes you on a journey to a place where you recognize who you truly are. Tune in to the mahogany if you wish to develop a sense of your divine self.

Oak

Almost everyone knows the oak and understands that it is strong and stable. I am blessed to live near some huge ancient oak trees. I hug them or stand with my back against them when I can. I can almost sense their wisdom, strength and endurance flowing into me. They are really special!

Over the years, humans have cut down so many wise old oaks that there are fewer left to do the work that many did in past times. Not only are there fewer oaks but there is more work to do. They are feeling tired and often dispirited. Every time you appreciate one, it helps them all to fulfil their divine mission.

Poplar

The poplar tree that graces so many roads and acts as a windbreak teaches us to be reliable, trustworthy and steady. When we internalize these qualities, people automatically trust us and depend on us.

Silver Birch

This is a tree of elegance, grace and charm. They send out the energy of harmony. At the same time they are vulnerable. Harmony with vulnerability opens your heart and this is their gift to humanity. Silver birches are heart openers, so they offer new beginnings and fertility.

Willow

This is a feminine water-loving tree that radiates an energy of flexibility. It is also a heart opener and brings romance. This is a very good tree to tune in to and make a wish from your heart.

Note that you can also do this at any time or place, whenever you see a tree. Call these energies in with a thought when you are out for a walk!

VISUALIZATION TO HELP THE TREES

1. Find a place where you can be quiet and undisturbed.
2. Call on Archangel Purlimiek, the angel of nature, and sense his beautiful green-blue energy.
3. Allow any tree to come into your mind's eye.
4. Bless it and thank it for coming to you.
5. Invoke the Gold Ray of Christ to pour down through the tree and spread through its roots.
6. Invoke the Lilac Fire of Source to pour down through the tree and spread out through its roots.
7. Invoke Archangel Michael's deep blue protective energy to pour down through the tree and spread out through its roots.
8. Invoke the Angel Mary's aquamarine light of divine feminine wisdom to pour down through the tree and spread out through its roots.
9. Invoke Archangel Sandalphon's silver light of balance and harmony to pour down through the tree and spread out through its roots.
10. Take a moment to invoke any energies you feel drawn to and see them flowing down through the tree.
11. Imagine the colours flowing from root to root, connecting the tree network and energizing the ley lines.
12. Open your eyes knowing you have helped the trees.

Conclusion

I have learned a huge amount about the natural world while writing this book and the more I know, the more I realize just how amazing and how precious animals, birds, fish, insects, reptiles and trees are. Without them we cannot exist.

The divine intention is that we coexist with the entire natural world and that we humans honour our fellow beings. Our spiritual contract on Earth is to live in total harmlessness with all. No animal has agreed to be eaten! When our energy fields are harmless towards another, they cannot hurt us. With our developed reasoning capacity, we are meant to be smoothing and easing their lives!

No animal, bird, insect, fish or reptile is near you by chance. Any one that is in your vicinity is attracted to your energy and is there for a purpose – often to teach you.

Many creatures are teaching us, often demonstrating to us by example. Have you noticed how sometimes a dog exhibits pure love by taking on its owner's illness? There are countless examples of these loyal animals staying to help their human companions, often sacrificing their own lives. An elderly acquaintance of mine fell while out walking with her dog on a local common. Night fell. It was cold. A search party could not find her. Eventually the barking of her dog, who had stayed by her side and cuddled up to her to keep her warm, led them to her in time to save her life.

Sometimes animals step away from their natural lives and allow themselves to be captured to try to help us develop compassion and understanding. There are many highly evolved animals in zoos or being used to raise money, who are sacrificing their lives to open our hearts. An animal chooses its incarnation and its lessons just as we do. How noble to be born into captivity so that humans can enjoy your beauty or satisfy our curiosity! Even more noble, actually beyond my comprehension, the animals who incarnate into laboratories to be experimented on. Is the life of a human more important than that of an animal?

We severely underestimate the insect kingdom. I really hope that this book will open people's eyes to their importance, quite apart from their tasks of breaking down matter and pollinating plants. A butterfly may be bringing you a message from the angels. If a bee is buzzing round you it is sending you healing. When a fly is buzzing irritatingly round you, ask if it is attracted to your undeclared anger, as well as reminding you to clean up.

Many creatures are serving our planet in beautiful ways, such as the pelicans and rhinoceroses who are holding the wisdom of the great civilization of Mu for us. The big cats are defending our planet from lower energies. Little rats are clearing our physical and psychic rubbish. Whales are keeping the frequency of the oceans high. Every creature is here for a purpose and plays a part in the great tapestry of life.

Birds are here to teach. They have nothing to learn. They demonstrate many qualities but mostly they show us how to be free and joyous. Every time you look into the sky and see a bird flying or gliding overhead, it is a reminder to set your consciousness free. Every time you listen to one singing, its song carries keys that remind you of who you truly are.

Reptiles still hold their original blueprint and remind us of the purity of being true to your divine essence.

Every variety of tree carries a quality that it can impart to you if you are ready to receive it. They are wise sentient beings, keepers of knowledge.

It is the birds, animals and fish who hold the frequency of the ley lines of our planet, along with the dragons and other etheric beings who serve Lady Gaia.

I do hope that this book has helped you to understand the natural world a little more though I am sure I have only scratched the surface of the secrets of nature.

You can do your part to help those we share our world with:

- Bless any creature you come across or think about. Each time you do so a spurt of higher energy touches them.

- When you acknowledge or thank an animal, bird, insect, reptile, fish or tree, it feels the energy of your notice and gratitude and is enlivened by it.

- Pray for the natural world. Every prayer is heard and makes a difference.

- Listen to the birds and absorb their messages.

- Be observant. What is the natural world teaching you?

Glossary of Terms

Gold Ray of Christ A ninth-dimensional energy of unconditional love.

Golden Age of Atlantis A 260,000 year civilization, known for incredible crystal technology.

Golden Age of Lemuria The Golden Age before Atlantis, when the beings were not physical and they particularly loved Earth and nature.

Golden Age of Mu This was the Age before Lemuria, when the beings were etheric and did not have physical bodies.

Golden Age of Petranium Petranium was the Golden Age of Africa.

Golden Ray The angelic ray, which is the colour gold.

Great Central Sun (Helios) This ninth-dimensional spiritual star sends light to Earth via our Sun.

Great Crystal The huge crystal that powered Atlantis.

Great Pyramid A pyramid built in Egypt after the fall of Atlantis.

Guardian angel the angel assigned to look after an individual.

Harmonic Convergence A significant alignment of stars and planets on 16 August 1987.

Hollow Earth The seventh-dimensional chakra in the centre of Earth.

Illumined One A being who holds great light.

Incarnate To be born into a physical body.

Incarnation A lifetime in a body of flesh.

Intergalactic Council The group of 12 beings who take decisions for the universe.

Intergalactic schools spiritual teaching establishments in the higher planes of the universe, attended by beings from all over the cosmos.

Jumbay the ascended aspect of the planet Jupiter.

Karma a spiritual debt.

Kundalini life-force energy stored in the base of the spine.

Kyhils Water elementals who help to consume the pollution in the oceans.

Lady Gaia The ninth-dimensional angel in charge of Earth.

Lakumay The ascended aspect of the star Sirius.

Lemurian crystals Crystals that were created by the beings of Lemuria.

Lemurians Those who existed in the great civilization of Lemuria.

Ley lines Energetic pathways that link places.

Lyran Stargate A gateway to the stars in the constellation of Lyra.

Magi Highly evolved and powerful priests.

Master Hilarion A great Master who ascended from Earth and is now in charge of the Ray of Science and Technology (the fifth ray).

Masters of Orion A council of wise beings which governs Orion.

Nigellay The ascended aspect of Mars.

Orb The sixth-dimensional aspect of an angelic being, which can be photographed.

Orion A constellation.

Oversoul A higher aspect of a group of souls in charge of their overall direction.

Pilchay The ascended aspect of our planet Earth.

Pleiades A star cluster.

Quishy The ascended aspect of the planet Saturn.

Retreat A space that vibrates with the energies of Archangels and Masters and is known as their home.

Seraphim Twelfth-dimensional angels.

Seraphina An angel who connects with humans.

Shekinah An evolved universe that vibrates at a tenth-dimensional frequency.

Solar plexus The spiritual centre or chakra at the solar plexus.

Sonics Sounds to which the angels add their energies.

Soul mission the assignment a soul undertakes for a lifetime.

Soul Star chakra The eleventh spiritual energy centre above the head.

Source The Creator, God.

Stellar Gateway The twelfth chakra that links us to the universe.

Step down Entering a space where you can lower your vibrational frequency.

Super moon A powerful moon that appears close to Earth and through which more divine feminine energy than usual is poured.

Sylph An air elemental.

Telepathic The ability to communicate mind to mind without speech.

Telephony The ascended aspect of the planet Mercury.

Third eye The chakra of enlightenment and clairvoyance situated in the centre of the forehead.

Third-dimensional frequency One of several low-dimensional frequencies at which people live from ego, selfishly and with closed hearts.

Throne A ninth-dimensional angel in charge of a planet or star.

Toutillay The ascended aspect of the Planet Neptune.

Ungrounded Not being energetically connected to the Earth.

Veil of Amnesia The seven layers between humans and God, in which we forget who we truly are.

ABOUT THE AUTHOR

Wayne Lawes

Diana Cooper received an angel visitation during a time of personal crisis. She is now well known for her work with angels, Orbs, Atlantis, unicorns, ascension and the transition to the new Golden Age. Through her guides and angels she enables people to access their spiritual gifts and psychic potential, and also connects them to their own angels, guides, Masters and unicorns.

Diana is the founder of The Diana Cooper Foundation, a not-for-profit organization that offers certificated spiritual teaching courses throughout the world. She is also the bestselling author of 28 books, which have been published in 27 languages.

www.dianacooper.com

HAY HOUSE

Look within

Join the conversation about latest products,
events, exclusive offers and more.

 Hay House UK

 @HayHouseUK

 @hayhouseuk

 healyourlife.com

We'd love to hear from you!

CPSIA information can be obtained
at www.ICGtesting.com
Printed in the USA
FSOW01n0130020617
34885FS